R E M E M B E R I N G   O L D

CHARLESTON

REMEMBERING OLD

CHARLESTON

A PEEK BEHIND PARLOR DOORS

Margaret Middleton Rivers Eastman

Charleston ⊢H⊣ London

THE
History
PRESS

Published by The History Press
Charleston, SC 29403
www.historypress.net

Copyright © 2008 by Margaret Middleton Rivers Eastman
All rights reserved

Back cover image: The Grove, seat of G.A. Hall, Esquire, circa 1800, by Thomas
Coram. © *Image Gibbes Museum of Art/Carolina Art Association.*

Cover design by Natasha Momberger

First published 2008
Second printing 2009
Third printing 2010

Manufactured in the United States

ISBN 978.1.59629.559.9

Library of Congress Cataloging-in-Publication Data

Eastman, Margaret M. R.
Remembering old Charleston : a peek behind parlor doors / Margaret
Middleton Rivers Eastman.
p. cm.
Includes bibliographical references.
ISBN 978-1-59629-559-9
1. Charleston (S.C.)--History--Anecdotes. 2. Charleston (S.C.)--Biography--
Anecdotes. I. Title.
F279.C457E36 2008
975.7'915--dc22
2008025671

In loving memory of Marwee Rivers and Edward Eastman,
for whom she started this book.
And to the kind friend who inspired me to finish these Charleston tales.

CONTENTS

ACKNOWLEDGEMENTS

Three years after my mother's death, I found the beginnings of a book:

> *I promised to execute this for my grandson when he was twenty.*
> *He grew up in the North and knows very little about his*
> *southern heritage. He wants to know more about the people in*
> *his background, not patriotic Revolutionary heroes, not the few*
> *who made contributions to our local history, but anecdotes and*
> *incidents of individuals and the accomplishments and quirks*
> *of his relatives and their acquaintances.*

Her unfinished work has been incorporated into this volume.

I want to thank the following people:

Dorothy Middleton Anderson, for contributing family photographs, reviewing the text and researching 24 New Street. I could not have produced this work without her assistance and encouragement.

Mendel Rivers, for his research on Governor James Hopkins Adams and Judge Waties Waring.

Philip A. Middleton, for providing information about the *Lelia*, his family remembrances and his research on the Heyward Washington House.

Acknowledgements

Major Alston Middleton, "our man in Bagdad," for reviewing Middleton material while on active duty.

Stuart Dawson, for introducing me to the Kennedy spy story, and Tootie Dawson, for Middleton family lore.

Beverly Stoney Johnson, for invaluable insights into the Kennedy connections with her grandfather's house.

George Abbott Middleton Jr., for providing many anecdotes in this volume.

Elizabeth Parker Dixon, for information about her Middleton grandparents' home.

Edward FitzSimons Good, for Trott family traditions and historical information.

Nancy Siegling Fortiere, for eyewitness recollections of the Meeting Street saga.

Charles Waring, for insights about his distinguished family.

Edith Corry, for interesting tidbits about Charleston.

Arla Holroyd, for editing the text and photographing me.

John White, Marie Ferrara, Rachael Allen, Angela Kleinschmidt, Anne Bennett and Claire Fund at the College of Charleston Special Collections Library, for their ongoing assistance.

Robert Stockton, for his wealth of knowledge and interest.

Jan Hiester, for images at the Charleston Museum.

Angela Mack, for images at the Gibbes Museum of Art.

St. Michael's Church, for the image of this historic treasure.

Seabrook Wilkinson, for helping with the second edition.

Others, for their help along the way: Laura All, Sy Baron, Jennie Hagen Boyd, Robert Eastman, Hayes Anderson Fordney, Lisa Claypoole Holland, Langhorne Howard, Marshall Hudson, Magan Lyons, Kara Mirmelstein, Natasha Momberger, Jaime Muehl, Katie Parry, Eleanor Campbell Peters, Ann FitzSimons Hull Platt, Vita FitzSimons Robertson, Carlton Simons, Hugh B. Tant III, Maurice (Molly) Eugenie Horne Thompson, Cambridge Trott, Joseph Trott III, Norman Walsh, Bradish J. Waring, Thomas Waring and Mary Bee Wilson.

INTRODUCTION

To appreciate these reminiscences, one must have some understanding of Charleston's history and how it influenced the inhabitants of this fair city. There was a brief time when Charleston was considered the richest colonial city on the Atlantic seaboard. It boasts many firsts: the first museum, the first drugstore, the first theatre, the first apartment building, the first shot fired in the Civil War, the first submarine. Charleston has seen feast and famine, victory and defeat, joy and grief.

The Carolina land grant was unique among the seventeenth-century colonial settlements in North America, be they Spanish, French or English. Carolina was presented to eight English supporters of Charles II in 1665. The colony was intended to be a buffer against the Spanish settlements farther south and to enrich the king's loyal supporters. The newly restored monarch was extremely generous, giving his friends what are now both of the Carolinas and Georgia, with a western boundary at the Pacific Ocean.

With such vast holdings, landed settlers from Barbados and other Caribbean islands quickly seized the opportunity to increase their fortunes. The Lords Proprietors gave the earliest arrivals an opportunity to become titled landholders. All they needed was enough money to buy the land. Depending on one's pocketbook, one might become a baron, a cacique or a landgrave.

Jane Margaret Simons Middleton, 1891–1980. *Courtesy Middleton family.*

A thriving aristocracy was soon established, for land could be grabbed up for a penny an acre. By the late seventeenth century, many bona fide members of the English and French aristocracies had joined the "first families." Merchants and artisans prospered and bought lands, soon becoming part of the ruling agrarian elite.

John Locke's *Fundamental Constitution* was written under the auspices of Lord Anthony Ashley Cooper but was never adopted, although some of its articles were incorporated into the colony's governing system. The religious tolerance for dissenters attracted Quakers, Jews, Baptists, Presbyterians and Huguenots, even though membership in the Church of England was the only vehicle for attaining political power.

In colonial times, Charleston's wealthy sons were usually educated in England. They played a major part in establishing the government of the United States. The city flourished for two centuries and set the pattern for the antebellum South, a region in which romance and chivalry were idealized. The aristocratic ideal established by Lord Anthony Ashley Cooper continued to flourish. Even the terrible upheavals of the War Between the States and the worse hardships of Reconstruction failed to alter the reverence for the social order desired by Charles II's eight cavaliers. If anything, Charleston became more caste conscious after "the War." One twentieth-century newsman quipped that Charlestonians "resemble the Chinese, who also drank tea, ate rice and worshiped their ancestors."[1]

In the twentieth century, Charleston's bluebloods gradually reestablished themselves in the lower end of the peninsular city, deserting neighborhoods that had once been fashionable. Although slums festered in some downtown streets, by the Roaring Twenties it was generally conceded that living below Broad Street was mandatory for social acceptability. Downtowners were caustically known by some as SOBs (South of Broad).

This volume is a collection of tales from the Middleton family; stories that were passed down as part of a cherished inheritance. Some of the information has already appeared in print elsewhere, but as cell phones, text messaging and other telecommunication devices replace the gentle art of conversation, this history is becoming lost. I acquired these stories through Margaret Middleton. She was the foremost authority on the itinerant colonial painter, Jeremiah Theus, and wrote biographies about Henrietta Johnson, America's first pastellist, and David and Martha Laurens Ramsay. Before her death, she wrote a romanticized story about Aphra Harleston and John Ball and a pamphlet about her family's adventures at Live Oak plantation.

A product of Victorian prudery, Margaret Middleton once wrote both the queen of England and the chief justice of the United States about their responsibility to set good examples during the time of moral decay in the United States (1958). She was a friend of Miss Sue Frost, an early preservationist, and was herself president of the Society for the Preservation of Old Dwellings long before it changed its name. She helped save the Heyward-Washington House on Church Street and the Glebe House, which is now the residence of the president of the College of Charleston. For her contributions to the community, Mrs. Middleton was presented the Roll of Honor by the Colonial Dames and was elected to the Hall of Fame by the Charleston Federation of Women's Clubs.

The Middleton daughters have published as well. Margaret Middleton Rivers's diaries have been used in historical research at the College of Charleston's Special Collections Library. She published *Fanfan* in 1984 and collaborated with her sister in preparing a second edition of *Jeremiah Theus*. Posthumous publications include *Verses by Marwee* and *Mendel and Me*. In addition to collaborating on the *Theus* reprint, Dorothy Middleton Anderson published family letters about blockade running in the *Bermuda Quarterly* and was elected to the Hall of Fame by the Charleston Federation of Women's Clubs exactly twenty years after her mother received the same honor.

Please turn back the clock and visit the spellbinding world of Charleston past.

–Margaret (Peg) Eastman
June 19, 2008

STREET MUSIC

Whenever you walk on a Charleston street
(Uneven flagstones or crumbling concrete),
You'd better be careful, for some aged square
Is waiting to trip you, if you're unaware.
The smaller squares say to each other, "It's fine
To see a pedestrian prone or supine."
The smooth-looking bigger ones seem to extend
A welcome to walkers—but you can't depend
On tricky antiquities in an old street.
While looking at houses, look out for your feet.
—Marwee Rivers à la A.A. Milne

For the most part, people have loved to visit Charleston, a delight that has been frequently chronicled by the numerous personages who have come to the Holy City. Long before the Morris Island lighthouse was built, the spire of St. Philip's Church served as the beacon that guided ships through the shoals and hidden currents of Charleston's narrow harbor entrance. It has been suggested that the sea-weary sailors who sighted Charles Towne's numerous church spires as they gradually appeared on the horizon were impressed by their number, and thus Charles Towne gained the name Holy City, in spite of its reputation to the contrary.

Or perhaps the name of the Holy City resulted from Locke's utopian constitution that granted religious freedoms to the early Carolina settlers. Whatever the origin, the name stuck. More recently, in November 2002, *Good Morning America* selected Charleston for a segment, and both Charles Gibson and Dianne Sawyer commented on Charleston's 750 churches, synagogues and mosques—an impressive number for a city of its size.

In the early twentieth century, visitors from "off" would sometimes stay at the handsome Villa Margherita on South Battery or the apartments in Berkeley Court by Colonial Lake. Regardless of their origins, these outsiders were called "rich Yankees," and they bought up the plantation lands and flocked to enjoy all that Charleston had to offer—and it had a lot to offer.

Both visitors and locals alike enjoyed taking leisurely strolls, and there were several charming locations available. The earliest and most loved, of course, was the Battery and White Point Gardens, popularly known by old-timers simply as "the park." At one time there were concerts in the park on Sundays. Vandals have forced the closing of the public facilities in White Point Gardens, but it was not always so.

There was also Colonial Lake, where young lovers could once court in rowboats, and little boys in white sailor suits could float their boats in competitions reminiscent of Renoir paintings. At the turn of the century, in the evenings young people would entertain themselves by walking around the lake, counting the number of gaslit street lamps reflected in the water. Hampton Park was another popular location that at one time had horse racing and was later known for its wonderful zoo.

Although there were setbacks after the Civil War, by the twentieth century the wealthy were back to partake in Charleston's milder climate and abundant winter flowers, camellias being a particular favorite. Springtime heralded millions of blossoms, the vivid hues of azaleas and the intoxicating smells of the tea olive and Confederate jasmine permeating the atmosphere like a heavy incense. Before the dinner hour at 2:00 p.m., passersby were tantalized by the inviting aromas of roasting beef or frying pork chops wafting through the open windows.

Charlie Middleton in his white sailor suit. *Courtesy Middleton family.*

In spite of its gentle climate and numerous attractions, Charleston was shabby throughout most of the twentieth century. Proud of their homes, owners made sure that the brass on their front doors was always gleaming, an accomplishment that required frequent polishing because of the humid salt air. The popular refrain, "too poor to paint and too proud to whitewash" had truth, as many of the houses boasted an abundance of chipped and peeling paint. It was the architecture that gave them charm.

By the Roaring Twenties, enterprising young black boys took advantage of the opportunity the visiting "rich Yankees" provided and danced for the coins tossed their way. It wasn't long before those entertaining gyrations were given a name, and "the Charleston" became wildly popular as people kicked up their heels to jazz music across the nation. Times were changing, and Charleston's young ladies joined in, enjoying the freedoms that followed earning the right to vote. Those flappers promptly cropped short both their hair and their skirts, and not all parents were enthusiastic about the new fads. A diary from that era notes: "How I hated to look like an angel or an old fashioned girl! Father insisted that I wear my hair long. All the other girls imitated modish flappers who had their hair shingled in Felder's Barber Shop."[2]

Before the Baby Boomer generation came along, courtly civility ruled the downtown streets. Gentlemen from the "old school" tipped their hats for the ladies, even the young girls. People dressed with decorum.

There was no graffiti, no broken beer bottles and no theft. Many storefront shops dotted downtown streets, with such names as Schweatmanns, Ohlandts and Burbages. Groceries were ordered by telephone and delivered to the door. There were schools, dry cleaners, filling stations and beauty shops within walking distance. It was a convenient, relaxed way of life.

Streets of earlier times had an infinite variety of attractions. Of course there were trolleys and the automobile, a new invention that attracted the local entrepreneurs. In mid-century, Mr. Wagner's horse-drawn carriages were available for an expensive

Young girls dressed with decorum even when playing on the cannons in White Point Gardens. *Courtesy College of Charleston Library (Rivers Family Collection).*

tour of the city, enticingly parked and waiting for hire on South Battery at the park.

Going to visit Fort Sumter was a pleasant excursion back when the dock was in the front of the Fort Sumter Hotel (now a condominium) and the harbor was not so congested. Walking tours became popular, and numerous ladies from the finest of Charleston homes proudly showed their city to visitors long before downtown streets were clogged with horse-drawn carriages and large groups of tourists.

One of the most picturesque sights was the street vendors hawking their wares. Some sold ice for the "ice boxes," while others sold vegetables, flowers and beautiful handmade baskets. Many women carried their wares in baskets balanced on top of their heads. Men pushed weather-beaten, makeshift carts decorated with chips of paint that had somehow managed to cling

Boat for hire in the thirties. *Courtesy College of Charleston Library (Rivers Family Collection).*

to the boards. Two large wheels at the back of the carts rolled them along, while a perpendicular board nailed to the front kept the carts from tipping over. Carts were used by shrimp and fish men, vegetable men and a peanut man as they roamed the streets, chanting their familiar refrains. They were beloved by the tourists and "old Charlestonians" alike. During the Azalea Festivals, vendors used to have competitions demonstrating their skills at White Point Gardens, and people crowded around to enjoy the show. Old-timers remember such ditties as:

> *Shark steak don't need no gravy,*
> *Two fish done killed my baby.*
> *Anyone want any porgy?*

The vendors were an institution, for Charleston has long been associated with Porgy, the endearing character made famous by DuBose Heyward in his novel *Porgy*, and later made immortal by George and Ira Gershwin in the folk opera *Porgy and Bess*. Of course, Charleston had a Catfish Row, located slightly south of Broad and just north of the historic Heyward-Washington House on Church Street.

The real Porgy was a cripple who moved around via goat cart. He had no access to downtown plumbing facilities and used a foul alley beside 49 Broad Street as a lavatory. People used to conjecture which smelled worse, Old Porgy or his goat. He didn't sing opera but chanted the same refrains as the other vendors.

The shrimp men had loud, mellifluous voices that would carry through open windows as they chanted in sing-song voices, "Swimpy, raw, raw, raw." If someone didn't have enough ready cash, they would lament, "Lady come to do-ah, wan-na buy. Have no money, so she go back 'n cry." Cooks would dash to the piazza and yell for "dem swimps," which were packed in ice and loaded on the pushcarts. In the thirties, the shrimp men sold shrimp for "fifteen cent a pie pan or a quartah fo' two," but by the early fifties, the carts had been modernized and "swimps" were weighed on scales suspended from crude wooden contraptions hammered to the cart frames.

Unusual accents were not confined to the street vendors. Children's nurses spoke that way, too. These nurses were called "Dah" (pronounced like "baa-baa" black sheep). They were invaluable members of Charleston's privileged households who disciplined, adored and spoiled their young charges. On nice afternoons, the Dahs gathered in the park (White Point Gardens), spreading their aprons and taking out their snuff or pipes as they gossiped while the children played. Sometimes Dahs terrified unruly children with threats of "Boo-Daddies" or "De Debbil."

Hard as it is to believe, the Middleton Dah had come to their family when she was about seventy years old. She remained with them for the next twenty years and then was "willed" to the growing family of a son who lived next door. By then she was about ninety. That old Dah continued to live in the servant's quarters at 10 Limehouse Street until she died. One of her treasures was a purple dress that she intended to be buried in. Her relatives came

Children with their "Dah," circa 1922. *Courtesy Middleton family.*

to pay respects to the corpse after her death, and later, when the body was being prepared for interment, it was discovered that someone had removed the garment from the trunk in which it had been lovingly kept for untold years.

The unusual speech of the black people has been called both Geechee and Gullah. It is a patois of English and the dialects of the African slaves who lived in the Lowcountry. One individual who was instrumental in preserving Gullah was Dick Reeves. He was a raconteur who was much in demand at banquets and other functions, always giving entertaining performances of well-loved Lowcountry stories. His recordings are valued for their humorous presentations and content. Many locals feel that Reeves helped keep Gullah alive as a separate language until the black community took an interest in preserving its rich heritage.

In addition, there was what is popularly known as the "old Charleston" accent, a more educated way of speaking that seems to have been influenced by settlers from the area of Newcastle, England. Descendants of those early settlers pronounce words like "mouse," "house," "out" and "about" in a manner still recognizable today. The "old Charleston" pronunciation of "late" and "eight" is unique. In the 1920s, Charles Middleton's accent once caused him to be recognized as a Charlestonian when he was overheard talking while in Italy. Back home, Charlestonians continued to "pack (park) their cyahs (cars) under the pam (palm) trees."

When the summer heat set in during the days before central air conditioning, anyone who could afford it left the city. Some may have vacationed in Newport, Rhode Island, but most went to the mountains of North Carolina or the numerous beaches near Charleston. Before Grace Memorial Bridge was constructed in 1929, one got to Sullivan's Island via a ferry to Mount Pleasant and then proceeded on a trolley over the causeway to the island.

Early in the twentieth century, the Middleton family had a house at Station 19, where the ocean breezes provided some relief from the hot, muggy, windless air in the city. Typical of the old, rambling

Mount Pleasant Ferry.
Courtesy Middleton family.

wooden beach houses, housekeeping was extremely inconvenient by today's standards. There were no electric appliances. A servant cooked on a wood stove in a detached kitchen and carried the food to the dining room. Large quantities of artesian drinking water were hauled from town, and household water was pumped on the piazza (Charlestonese for porch). Groceries were kept in a closet in the dining room.

A few enterprising summer residents, like the Andersons at Station 27, kept a cow and chickens on the island for the family commissary. Ice cream was made at home, and happy children vied for the pleasure of adding the rock salt and turning the handle.

Clothing must have been uncomfortable by today's standards, for beach goers wore bathing costumes that covered up most of the body, and children's bathing suits were often made of knitted

Bathing costumes, circa 1910. *Courtesy Middleton family.*

bouclé wool yarn, which youngsters complained felt like "torture" when wet. Then, of course, the mosquitoes took a bite whenever they could.

There were, however, many pleasant recollections of the island:

> *Memories are of cool breezes, laughter and song. A lovely cool, shady back porch and a tremendous ice chest always brimming with luscious fruits and vegetables...children building sandcastles under the house where they played contentedly for hours when not on the beach...plenty of servants to cook and wash the dishes and replenish water in the pitchers on every washstand...We would all gather every afternoon and meet the trolley when Father came home and help him carry his packages. For many years, ice and groceries had to be brought over from the city. His first words were always the same: "Thank Heavens to be back on the Island—it was hot as Hades in town today." Then we would all go for a dip, which was called a "bath" in those days.*[3]

THE CROWN JEWEL OF
LOWER CHURCH STREET

The Heyward Washington House

Everybody loves Church Street. Capped by the magnificent St. Philip's Church, this quaint crooked street snakes its way down the lower Charleston peninsula to White Point Gardens. Of the many historical buildings, the most prestigious by far is number 87, the handsome brick residence of Thomas Heyward Jr., signer of the Declaration of Independence. Later, President George Washington lodged there during his week-long visit to Charleston in 1791. After occupation by Union troops, the house gradually declined, and it was eventually turned into a bakery and further defaced by the addition of a storefront and additional entrance door on the ground floor.

The dear "little old ladies" who founded the Society for the Preservation of Old Dwellings valued Charleston's rich historical and architectural heritage at a time when many elegant colonial mansions across the nation were giving way to the ravages of neglect and poverty. Those farsighted women were instrumental in preserving *in situ* this national treasure at a time when wealthy collectors from elsewhere were buying, dismantling and relocating historically significant buildings. In 1929, the Charleston Museum purchased the property with the assistance of the Society for the Preservation of Old Dwellings, making it the first historic house museum in Charleston. It has since been placed on the National Historic Register.

The Heyward-Washington House after the bakery window and doorway were removed and the original façade was restored. *Courtesy the Charleston Museum, Charleston, South Carolina.*

Although today 87 Church is called the Heyward-Washington House, in 1776 it was the recently constructed home of Thomas Heyward. The dwelling is located on the site of a house built around 1740 by a well-to-do gunsmith. It passed hands to Colonel Daniel Heyward, a rice planter who had purchased the property in 1770 from Roger Pinckney, the provost marshal. The elder Heyward gave the property to his son Thomas, who had recently returned from studying law in England.

Young Heyward razed the existing house and in 1772 began construction of an elegant, three-story, brick double house with a central hall. Heyward kept the dependencies at the rear of the property, where they have remained intact to this day.[4]

Heyward married Elizabeth Matthewes, a regional beauty from a well-established colonial family. Heyward's brother-in-law, John Matthewes, was a dedicated legislator, jurist, Patriot and governor of South Carolina who also served the state in other prominent capacities. Heyward's sister-in-law, Lois, married George Abbott Hall, a prominent merchant who had emigrated from Bristol, England, some years earlier.

Like his brothers-in-law, Heyward was active in local politics. He served in the House of Commons, the first and second Provincial Congresses and ultimately as a member of the South Carolina delegation in the Second Continental Congress in Philadelphia in 1776. When young Heyward returned after signing the Declaration of Independence, his father was reported to have expressed his indignation along these lines:

> *"A bold and precipitate measure I think. Undisciplined militia like ours cannot stand against the trained armies of the king. We shall surely be beaten."*
> *"No doubt," was the reply.*
> *"What shall we do then?"*
> *"Raise another army and keep up the struggle."*
> *"What, to be beaten again?"*
> *"Certainly, and the same may follow over and over again; but we shall become reconciled to the evils of war and acquiring military experience, shall ultimately gain the victory."*[5]

After the British captured Charles Town in May 1780, Heyward, then a captain in the Charleston Artillery Company, and Hall, a captain in the First Battalion of the South Carolina militia, surrendered their swords and gave their parole not to offend the enemy. In spite of being gentlemen, they were rudely accosted by the British officers with filth and insults.

In August 1780, Heyward was among forty-three Charles Town Patriots whom the British seized and sent to the Spanish fort at St. Augustine, Florida. Hall was among a group of twenty-two civic and military leaders who were sent there in November. Heyward is reported to have been a cheerful fellow, who boosted the morale of his fellow prisoners with his jokes and mirthful songs.

Meanwhile, in Philadelphia, John Matthewes worked with the Continental Congress to pass a bill authorizing an exchange of prisoners. Matthewes personally petitioned George Washington to assist the Southern leaders sent to St. Augustine. Washington wrote him that a solution was difficult, because the British prisoners were of inferior rank, remarking in his letter of February 26, 1781:

Your favor of the 15ᵗʰ was not received till this morning. I am so totally unacquainted with the state of the Southern prisoners that I did not choose to enter into a negotiation with Sir Henry Clinton on the idea of a general exchange although liberty was given me by Congress. Nothing particular has therefore been done respecting the gentlemen who are confined at St. Augustine, as it could not be supposed that the enemy would consent to a partial exchange of persons of the most considerable influence in the southern states, and who besides are pretended to have rendered themselves obnoxious. Indeed, whenever a negotiation is entered upon, I foresee difficulties in procuring the liberation of those gentlemen, who are most of them eminent in the civil line, as we have none of similar rank in our possession to exchange for them. However, when the matter is gone into, you may be assured that all possible attention shall be paid to them, not only from my own inclination to serve them but in obedience to an act of Congress which directs that particular regard shall be had to them in the negotiation of the exchanges of southern prisoners. The interest you take in them will be an additional consideration.

It was some months before those held in St. Augustine were exchanged and taken to Philadelphia. In Charles Town, after their husbands were exiled to St. Augustine, the Matthewes sisters and their children remained at 87 Church Street. They had to endure all types of harassment and privation, and their misadventures have been passed down for generations.

When the British ordered that the city celebrate the British victory at Guilford, Elizabeth Heyward, a proud and spirited woman, refused. She was reputed to have been a woman of remarkable beauty and personal grace. She also had an indomitable will and the feisty deportment of many of the South Carolina women of the Revolution. She had all the windows tightly shuttered, although both sisters knew the horrors of the Provost, a dungeon where criminal and political prisoners were herded together in a foul state of neglect.

A British officer came to the door and demanded that Mrs. Heyward place candles in the windows of her home.

"Can I celebrate your victory while my husband is a prisoner at St. Augustine?"

"That is of little consequence," said the officer. "Greene is defeated and the last hopes of the rebellion are crushed; you shall illuminate."

"Not a light," was the reply.

"Then I will return and level your house to the ground."[6]

Elizabeth Heyward stood firm. The stress of this incident seriously affected her sister, who was expecting her twelfth child, three having died previously. Lois Hall began to decline.

May 12, 1781, was the anniversary of the capture of Charles Town, and the British once again gave orders for the city to celebrate and illuminate. Once again the Heyward mansion remained dark. This time an unruly mob stormed the home "with brickbats and every species of nauseating trash that could offend or annoy"[7] while trying to force entry. Inside, the violence took its toll. Lois Hall died in childbirth during the mayhem.

After the incident, the British apologized and offered to repair the damage, but the proud and bereaved Elizabeth Heyward refused their offer, preferring to have the damage remain as a visible testimony of the British failure to protect her home.[8] No record remains of whether the unfortunate Lois Hall had yet been buried when the apology was made.

In June 1781, George Abbott Hall returned to Charles Town to secure passage for his sister-in-law, her son and his numerous children. They sailed to Philadelphia on a prisoner ship called a cartel. The extended family was reunited, and the three brothers-in-law continued to work for the Continental cause.

The next year, Elizabeth Heyward was honored by General Washington, who selected her as the Queen of Love and Beauty at a Philadelphia ball given in honor of the birth of the Dauphin of France. Throughout the vicissitudes of British occupation, the resolute Elizabeth had remained true to patriotic principles. And like her sister, the years of hardship caused her health to wane. She did not live long in exile, dying in Philadelphia in August 1782.[9]

Thomas Heyward returned to South Carolina after the British evacuated and remarried four years later. He spent most of his time on his plantation and rented his Church Street town house to the city so that George Washington could stay there when he visited Charleston in May 1791. At the time of Washington's visit, Heyward was remodeling the kitchen dependency, and there are two traditions about the arrangements. One was that Washington made some suggestions about what should be done, and the other was that food was cooked across the street at number 86 because the kitchen was so modern. Heyward sold the property to John Faucheraud Grimké in 1794.[10]

Grimké fought with distinction on the colonial side during the Revolution and was imprisoned by the British, but he later escaped and joined General Nathanael Greene, serving under him until the end of the conflict. He was also a cotton planter, legislator and a distinguished jurist who served on the South Carolina bench for thirty-six years. His impartiality did much to heal concerns of the upstate Tories after the British left. He stated, "We are all Americans" and claimed that "our passions" were the only enemy of legal justice.[11]

In 1784, Grimké published a guideline for the officers of the new judiciary, and in 1790 he published an updated digest of state laws, providing the basis for judiciary uniformity and professionalism of legal study. He introduced provisions to ensure separation of the judiciary from the legislature at the State Constitutional Convention.

Grimké produced fourteen children, including two well-known abolitionists, Sarah Moore Grimké and Angelina Emily Grimké. According to local traditions, the Grimké sisters learned to hate the injustices of slavery as children by watching their domineering father's treatment of a mulatto half brother, the son of a slave, who was forced to serve the family. In addition, their mother was a superintendent of the Ladies Benevolent Society and introduced her daughters to charitable works and to the privations of poverty among white and freed black women. Both of the outspoken sisters must have acquired the indomitable spirit of their father, for they became pariahs in Charleston because of their strident stance against slavery in the 1820s. Both women moved North and never returned to Charleston. They became politically active suffragettes after slavery was abolished.

J.F. Grimké died in 1819, and 87 Church Street became a boardinghouse run by his aunt, Mrs. Rebecca Jameson. In 1824, it was purchased by Mrs. Margaret Munro, who also operated a boardinghouse.[12] Margaret Munro left the house to her granddaughter, Elizabeth Jane Hervey,[13] who married Tobias Cambridge Trott in 1857.

Like the previous owners, the Trott family had a proud lineage going all the way back to England, where John Trott, a draper, was awarded a coat of arms by Queen Elizabeth in the sixteenth century. John West Trott, whose descendants lived at 87 Church Street, was the brother of the Proprietary Judge Nicholas Trott.

Judge Trott was not only a political power, but he was also a highly acclaimed scholar and jurist. Much has already been written about Judge Trott elsewhere, but among other accomplishments, Trott codified South Carolina law, the first book printed in the colony in 1736.

Because of his close ties with the Lords Proprietors, Nicholas Trott ran into difficulties politically. He was regarded as being an overbearing and contentious man, but regardless of his reputation, there once was a street named after him in Charleston. According to local tradition, it was located at the east end of the present-day Wentworth Street. In 1709, Trott built a stuccoed office building and an exposed brick house beside the old powder magazine, buildings that have survived the numerous city fires since that time.

As the vice admiralty judge, Trott presided over the trial of the notorious "gentleman" pirate Stede Bonnet. Colonel William Rhett had captured and assisted in the prosecution of Bonnet. Nicholas Trott and William Rhett were closely connected by marriage, as Rhett's son was married to Trott's daughter.

William Rhett built a handsome home that was completed shortly before his death in 1722. Judge Trott married his widow in 1730 and moved from his more modest house that tradition states was next to the powder magazine into his wife's new, and much safer, uptown home, whereupon the Rhett property was briefly called "Trott's Point." (William Rhett's house on Hasell Street is the birthplace of South Carolina's beloved Wade Hampton.)

There is a poignant footnote to the Trott ownership of the Heyward-Washington House. The newlyweds resided at 87 Church Street after their marriage. Tobias Cambridge Trott died unexpectedly six years later. According to the December 29, 1863 obituary in the *Charleston Daily Courier*:

> *We are startled on being informed of the death of Mr. T. Cambridge Trott who has been for some years well known as the Book-keeper and financial manager in the* Mercury *office. He left his post some ten days ago to visit his family in Columbia, complaining a little, but otherwise in health as far as his friends knew. He died on Sunday of Typhoid fever. Our sympathies however unavailing in such a case, are due and are tendered to the office of the* Mercury *and still more to the sorely bereaved family, a wife and three children. Mr. Trott was in the 31st year of his age.*

Cambridge Trott's untimely death was accentuated by the hardships of war. According to the family, Trott's bereaved young family refugeed upstate during the Union bombardment of Charleston. After the city fell, Union soldiers were billeted at 87 Church.

The Trott family has a charming tradition that when the Union troops finally left, someone in the departing army reportedly "gave" the house to a former slave housekeeper named Mamu. Now, Elizabeth Trott was reputed to have been a woman far ahead of her times. Like the Grimké sisters before her, she had compassion for those who were bound to her service and educated her slaves, something rarely done in the antebellum South. Although Mamu could not have possibly been sophisticated enough to understand land conveyances, she did understand that the house belonged to her former mistress. So, Mamu wrote a letter after the soldiers departed, notifying her mistress that she could have the house back. It is interesting to note that Mamu knew exactly where to contact her. It should also be mentioned that many Southern families had strong bonds with their slaves, and many freed blacks expected their former owners to look out for them long after the destruction of war and Reconstruction were part of the past.

At the close of the war, things were difficult for the young widow. Money was scarce, and almost everyone had been bankrupted.

Elizabeth Trott was living on Church Street when she tried to raise some money by selling a silver coffee urn with a spirit lamp beneath. C.E. Chichester of Number 1 Atlantic Street was so moved by sympathy for the young widow and her little children that in spite of a "slight" dent in the side of the urn, he purchased it for the ten-dollar asking price. Thirty years later, Chichester wrote her son, Major Cambridge Munro Trott, to inquire if he would like to buy it back, as it had not been used for more than twenty years. Cambridge Trott acquired the urn and decided to have it restored. A local antique dealer sent the urn to New York, where it mysteriously disappeared, never to be seen again.

The *Charleston Courier* reported that Elizabeth Trott married Howard P. Cooke in the bride's home on March 28, 1868. A prenuptial agreement ensured that 87 Church Street went into trust if Cooke predeceased his wife and to the Trott children if she died.[14]

Number 87 Church Street passed out of the Trott trust in 1879, when the last trustee died, and the property was sold to Elizabeth Wehrhan for $3,500.[15] By the late nineteenth century, the building had been purchased for $5,000 by Henry W. Fuseler[16] and had been converted into a bakery with a first-floor storefront. The defaced building survived until the Society for the Preservation of Old Dwellings got involved, at which time it was acquired by the Charleston Museum.[17]

As the memories of history fade, it is good to remember that the Heyward-Washington House was occupied by many champions of liberty and justice. Each generation of residents of this remarkable house left an indelible mark on history. An unheralded jewel in the crown is surely Elizabeth Jane Trott, whose story has been overshadowed by greater luminaries. Elizabeth's generous spirit personifies the essence of noblesse oblige and that unwritten code by which the Southern aristocracy lived and died.

The Heyward-Washington House is reputed to have a ghost, and the reader can fancy which of its many residents still paces the floors, championing the cause of liberty.

THE PATRIOT

The Grove Plantation, Now Lowndes Grove

Even though he played a prominent role during the Revolution and paid dearly for his patriotism, George Abbott Hall is one of the men history seems to have neglected. He was a merchant from Bristol England who immigrated to the Carolinas in the 1750s and was recorded as owning land by the 1760s. The Hall family was of some substance in England, for Hall had a partner, a Mr. Wraxall, whom he mentioned in his will. The Hall arms have been preserved in a silver christening bowl and in George Abbott Hall's bookplate.

Hall married into the Carolina landed aristocracy. His wife's great-grandfather had been the controversial Proprietary Governor Robert Gibbes, whose lineage can be traced all the way back to 1574.[18] In 1719, the governor's son, Colonel John Gibbes, married Mary Woodward, granddaughter of the beloved explorer and Indian agent Henry Woodward. Their daughter, Sarah, married John Matthewes in 1741.

John and Sarah Matthewes had four children. Their son John served in the legislative bodies of the colony and the state and served as state governor. The Matthewes sisters married well. Elizabeth married Thomas Heyward Jr., signer of the Declaration of Independence, Ann married Godin Guerard and Lois married George Abbott Hall.

The Halls were wed in St. Paul's Parish, Stono, in 1764. A year after their marriage, the young couple sailed to England with their infant daughter, Elizabeth. Three more children had been born by the time the young family returned to Charles Town in 1769.

Once back in South Carolina, the energetic George Abbott Hall became actively involved in local politics. His name was second on a list signed by citizens who refused to import British goods. When the Provincial Assembly formed a patriotic association, Hall was a committeeman, and within four days, nearly every man in Charles Town had joined. From November 1, 1775, to March 26, 1776, Hall was a member of the Second Provincial Congress of South Carolina, as were his brothers-in-law Thomas Heyward and John Matthewes.

In 1776, military preparations began. Hall was on the commission to outfit and arm vessels, to raise £100,000 for two artillery regiments and to outfit three infantry regiments and a regiment of rangers. He also served in the South Carolina General Assembly and was on a board to direct South Carolina naval affairs.[19] He was appointed to a committee to buy rice to raise

George Abbott Hall. *Courtesy College of Charleston Library (Rivers Family Collection).*

money to purchase clothing for the troops. That same year, Hall was appointed the customs collector for the port of Charles Town, a position that he held continuously until his death in 1791.

Hall's services were not limited to civilian activities, for he was also a captain of the First Battalion of South Carolina militia and presided at a court-martial held in Thomas Heyward's house on Church Street.[20]

In May 1780, Charles Town fell into the hands of the British. Historian McCrady's account eloquently states that Charles Town was "the only city in America to endure a British siege during the war, and [was] ruled by Balfour, an officer who reserved his valor for the oppression of defenseless men, unprotected women, and innocent children."[21] When the British finally captured the city, John Matthewes was safely in Philadelphia, but his brothers-in-law did not fare so well.

Alexander Garden's *Anecdotes of the Revolutionary War* relates that after they had surrendered their swords and had given their parole not to offend the enemy, Heyward and Hall were rudely accosted on the street by British officers who snatched the cockades from their hats and trampled them on the ground, "while they pelted the prisoners with filth and insulted them with ribaldry."[22]

Although the civil and military leaders of South Carolina were supposed to have been guaranteed personal security, sixty-five prominent citizens were arrested and taken to St. Augustine, Florida. Hall was among the more fortunate group of detainees as they were permitted to live in rented quarters and enjoy the services of the servants they were allowed to bring with them.[23]

This breach of good faith by the British caused a lot of consternation in Philadelphia, where John Matthewes was trying to get the prisoners released. Congress passed a bill authorizing an exchange, and General Washington was personally petitioned. Unfortunately, the Continentals had British prisoners of inferior rank, and it took several months to secure an exchange.

Hall was released on June 22 and permitted to return to occupied Charles Town because of his wife's death in May.

There he gathered his grieving children and the beautiful Elizabeth Heyward and sailed to Philadelphia in a foul ship that was used to transport prisoners. They arrived in December after a journey that must have been extremely difficult for everyone, especially young Elizabeth Hall, who was barely sixteen when she was forced to assume care of her eight siblings, the youngest only a five-month-old infant.[24]

Hall and Heyward joined their brother-in-law John Matthewes in Philadelphia and dedicated themselves to the American cause for the next two years. As chairman of the committee at headquarters, John Matthewes had worked with George Washington to organize the Continental army and was instrumental in securing the appointment of General Nathanael Greene to replace General Horatio Gates as the commander of the Southern army.

While in Philadelphia, Hall worked with Robert Morris, the financier of the Continental government, and was appointed receiver of taxes for South Carolina. (They were the most important representatives of the confederation in each state; Alexander Hamilton had the same assignment for New York.) The receivers were entrusted with fulfilling quotas of revenue, preventing the states from issuing inflationary paper money and sending Morris reports on commerce, economy and political affairs of their states. Robert Morris devised a plan for the receivers to issue notes, but it was strongly resisted by Congress and was one of the issues leading to the Constitutional Convention of 1787.[25]

As receiver, Hall returned to South Carolina by land, taking with him a wagon train of supplies for Southern regiments. He was instructed to return with indigo, skins or furs. When none were to be had, Morris requested that rice be shipped directly from Carolina to the Amsterdam bankers as a payment for South Carolina's tax assessments.[26]

Hall also delivered funds to General Greene, commander of the Southern colonial army. This assignment led to certain misunderstandings between Greene and Morris, as well as the public embarrassment of General Greene, for a greedy British merchant named John Banks had tried to corner the market on clothing before he fled Charleston after the British troops were withdrawn. Greene's association with Banks was exploited in the press, and the repercussions haunted him for years. Reports of the mysterious stranger caused contemporary writers to imply that Mr. Morris did not trust General Greene.[27]

The embarrassing matter was not cleared up until after the Revolution, when General Greene and the "Financier" chatted in Morris's office. Greene remarked that twice he felt there had been divine intervention on his behalf during the war. With a twinkle in his eye Morris asked for an explanation.

> *On one occasion, I was seated in my tent, overwhelmed with gloomy apprehensions. My army, I felt, must be disbanded unless they could obtain food, clothing and other supplies. At the battle of Eutaw Springs some of my men were as naked as they day they were born. They could not fight on against such odds. As I was thus lost in gloomy reflections, I was suddenly approached by a gentleman I had seen occasionally around camp, who placed at my command £30,000 on my personal note and made payable to you as Minister of Finance.*

Morris remained silent as Green related another occasion when the unknown stranger had appeared, supplied funds to the army and then vanished as mysteriously as he had come. (Greene had solicited from his unknown benefactor an advance to cover a demand of 1,200 guineas cash and an £8,000 note on Morris. This immense sum depleted the resources Hall had at his disposal.)

Enjoying Greene's narrative, Morris smiled and told him that the mysterious visitor was none other than George Abbott Hall, whom he employed to provide for his army when it most needed funds. To which Greene indignantly replied, "Then, sir, you did not trust me." Morris warmly assured him that if money had been sent directly to Greene, it would have been spent immediately and nothing would have been available when the army needed funds to survive.[28]

After the British evacuation, George Abbott Hall returned to Charleston. Through his deceased wife's family, Hall acquired a tract of land called "The Grove," where he built a home for his large family.

Like its owners, The Grove has an interesting history.

John Gibbes, Lois Hall's grandfather, had purchased the Ashley River property in 1769, when he also obtained a grant to the adjacent marshland. Gibbes built a handsome residence on what became known as Orange Grove plantation because of his attempt to grow Seville oranges. Although South Carolina's climate was too harsh for the citrus endeavor to be successful, a derivative of the plantation's name stuck, hence "The Grove."

In addition to an orange grove, Gibbes cultivated an extensive garden of exotic plants, complete with a greenhouse and a pinery for pineapples. It was described by the invading Hessian officers as being "one of the most beautiful pleasure gardens in the world."[29]

Alexander Garden reported that the British troops under Major General Augustine Provost destroyed The Grove during an unsuccessful attack on Charleston in 1779. John Gibbes was considered an "arch Rebel." During the attack, he was staying at his invalid brother's plantation on the Stono River, even though it, too, was occupied by a considerable British force. Upon hearing of the destruction of The Grove, Gibbes, a man of "strong passions," indignantly cursed the scoundrel who struck the first blow to his precious trees. Fortunately for the old gentleman, the British commander let the matter drop. That evening, because of the dreadful catastrophe, Mr. Gibbes drank to an unaccustomed "intemperance." He went to bed and died in his sleep.[30]

Hall built another impressive dwelling near the burned-out site of Gibbes's mansion. Overlooking the river, the new house was located at the end of what is now St. Margaret Street. Hall's property later became known as Lowndes Grove after it was acquired by U.S. Congressman William Lowndes in 1804. Still surrounded by stately oaks, this elegant home is considered the last surviving plantation house on the peninsula to be located on enough open ground to provide the illusion of a rural setting.

It has been suggested that The Grove was where the famous duel between General Christopher Gadsden and General Robert Howe took place, although other accounts claim that the duel occurred on the property of William Percy near Rutledge Avenue and Bogard Street.

Regardless of the venue, the conflict between the two men escalated because the firebrand, Charles Town–born Gadsden, resented North Carolina's Howe being given command of the South Carolina Continental troops. Gadsden objected to Howe's management of the military in Georgia in 1778 so strongly that he protested to both the Continental Congress and the South Carolina General Assembly and resigned his commission. Chagrined that his resignation was accepted after the prominent role he had played in South Carolina's government, Gadsden insisted upon a duel to satisfy his honor. General Howe fired first

The Grove, seat of G.A. Hall, Esquire, circa 1800, by Thomas Coram.
© *Image Gibbes Museum of Art/Carolina Art Association.*

and missed, whereupon Gadsden took his time and deliberately fired into some nearby trees, much to everyone's relief. Afterward, the generals shook hands and parted.

This celebrated duel appeared in newspapers just four days after it occurred. As far away as New York City, Major André, the famous British spy, wrote a parody of the event, much to the delight of the British and the annoyance of the colonials. (Gadsden is remembered for being the only colonial leader to have been imprisoned in the dungeon at St. Augustine and for designing the yellow flag with a coiled rattlesnake poised over the words "Don't Tread on Me.")[31]

When Sir Henry Clinton's troops invaded the Charles Town Neck in 1780, they unloaded their materiel at John Gibbes's boat landing and made various encampments on his land during their attack on the city. The first skirmish of the siege of Charles Town in March 1780 was at the junction of the road to The Grove and what is now King Street.

On May 5, 1789, upon the recommendation of the Honorable Edward Rutledge, President Washington appointed George Abbott Hall to be the first federal port collector in the Custom House. Washington wrote Rutledge:

> *I anticipate that one of the most difficult and delicate parts of the duties of my office will be that which relates to nominations for appointments. I receive with more satisfaction the strong testimonials in behalf of Mr. Hall, because I hope they will tend to supersede difficulty in this instance.—Nothing could be more agreeable to me than to have one candidate brought forward for every office with such clear pretensions as to secure him against competition.*[32]

George Abbott Hall was port collector until his death on August 1, 1791. He left behind a large family and a well-deserved good name for his exemplary and honest public service.

INVASION OF
PEACEFUL RETREAT

A John's Island Plantation

Two of the early Carolina settlers from Barbados were Colonel John Godfrey and Dr. Henry Woodward, who was one of the most fascinating pioneers our country has produced. Woodward married Godfrey's daughter Mary, and among their descendants are many famous Charlestonians. Woodward is one of the most beloved of the early colonists. A commemorative plaque about his accomplishments is located at Magnolia Gardens. Marwee Rivers, a Charleston tour guide, always claimed that the reason Henry Woodward was not as famous as Daniel Boone was "because Yankees wrote the history books."

Dr. Woodward accompanied Robert Sanford on the exploratory voyage sent out by the Lords Proprietors. He volunteered to stay behind with the Indians of Carolina in 1666, four years before Charles Towne was founded. He learned the native language, and the Indians taught him the lore of the virgin wilderness and later saved the colony from starvation.

When a Spanish expedition learned of Woodward's presence in what they considered to be their territory, he was captured and imprisoned in the fort at St. Augustine. Two years later, the British privateer Robert Searle sacked St. Augustine. Woodward escaped and joined the privateer as ship's surgeon. Returning to the Carolinas, Woodward worked among Indians for the Lords Proprietors and established trading routes as far west as the Mississippi. He contracted an illness during one of his westward explorations and died in 1690, leaving behind a wife and three children.

In 1719, Henry Woodward's daughter Mary married Colonel John Gibbes, son of the late Governor Robert Gibbes. The governor was a very ambitious man who came from a well-connected family in England. Gibbes and his brother joined in the early settlement of Barbados and later collaborated with the Lords Proprietors to develop the Carolinas. He was capable and participated in the early colonization of the land grant, commuting back and forth to Barbados frequently.

Gibbes was part of the governing assembly in the unsuccessful attempt to settle Cape Fear, and by the 1670s he had acquired large quantities of land in the Carolinas. He served in the colonial government in various capacities, including sheriff and as a representative in what became the Commons Assembly House. He was the Colleton family's deputy and was appointed chief justice of the colony in 1710. After the colonial governor died that same year, he became governor under extremely suspicious circumstances. His alleged misdeeds soon came to light and nearly caused a civil war. The colonial government practically ceased to function while word of his actions was sent to the Lords Proprietors.

In 1711, Governor Gibbes sent Colonel John Barnwell to North Carolina to help save the colony from the Tuscarora Indian uprising. Governor Gibbes also had the foresight to realize the need for more white settlers to offset the huge black population being imported into the colony. In 1711, he made a speech to the Commons House, warning against the growing slave trade and its associated problems.

The Lords Proprietors replaced Gibbes with Charles Craven in 1712 and withheld his salary as colonial governor. Gibbes died in 1715. [33]

By the time of the Revolution, the Gibbes family was well established and owned a great deal of land. They enjoyed the amenities of city life and their country estates. One of the governor's descendants was another Robert Gibbes. He had a home in Charles Town, but spent the bulk of his time on John's Island at a plantation called Peaceful Retreat, about a two-hour sail from Charles Town. It was an elegant estate. The grounds were beautifully laid out with shaded walks and a view of the water. In addition to the usual outbuildings and quarters for the servants, the property boasted a brick mansion built in the English tradition, with a portico facing the Stono River. Flanking the house were a two-story kitchen and office building and a matching school building, both of which were connected to the main house by an open fence. Peaceful Retreat was known throughout the area for its genteel lifestyle, hospitality and good taste.

Robert Gibbes had been so crippled by gout that his movement was confined to a chair on wheels. Due to this disability, he was unable to participate in war, but like many of the landed aristocracy he had sympathies for the patriotic cause and warmly entertained those who shared his views. Gibbes was married to Sarah Reeve, his second wife. She was a capable and charming woman who had devoted herself to the management of the plantation while caring for her infirm husband and eight children. In addition, she had the guardianship of the seven orphaned

Mrs. Robert Gibbes's place, John's Island, from untitled sketchbook (1796–1805) by Charles Fraser. © *Image Gibbes Museum of Art/Carolina Art Association.*

children of her husband's deceased sister, Mrs. Fenwick. (Fenwick Place was located three miles from Peaceful Retreat.)

Pleasant Retreat's reputation for luxurious living was its undoing. By the beginning of 1780, Georgia had fallen to the British forces and Sir Henry Clinton turned his attention to the conquest of Charles Town. Admiral Mariot Arbuthonot's fleet had blockaded Charles Town harbor, and the invading British forces had overrun the surrounding countryside. There are varying accounts of how a group of British and Hessian soldiers invaded Peaceful Retreat. Elizabeth Ellet's account was obtained from a granddaughter of Mrs. Gibbes.[34]

According to Ellet, the British decided to make the Gibbes plantation their headquarters on the Stono River. They arrived by boat in the dead of night and stealthily surrounded the house. An aged servant awoke his mistress and told her of the soldiers. Mrs. Gibbes hastily dressed herself and awakened several ladies who were visiting at the time.

Perhaps one of her guests was Susanna Matthewes Hall, the first cousin of the four Matthewes siblings. She was married to George Abbott Hall's younger brother Daniel.[35] A defiant rebel in her own right, her wit and saucy tongue had earned her quite a reputation among the British officers. During the British occupation, against the advice of her husband, Susanna Hall attended a dinner in Charles Town at which a young lady gave a toast "to the blood that flowed at Guilford." To which Mrs. Hall immediately responded, "Thank god the blood of the British washed away that of the Americans," and made a hasty departure thereafter. Susanna Hall smuggled letters on her person to the American troops near Charles Town. Once, when traveling to John's Island with a boatload of supplies for the troops,[36] she passed herself off as a dying woman visiting her mother. As tradition goes, a British officer on the dock demanded the key to her trunk. When she inquired why, he replied that he wished "to inspect for treason, madam." The spirited Mrs. Hall replied, "Then you may be saved the trouble of search, for you may find enough of it at my tongue's end."[37]

As she was dressing, Mrs. Gibbes wisely conjectured that everyone in the house would be treated better if the enemy realized that it was inhabited solely by helpless women and children who were unable to defend themselves. The servants quickly dressed all of the children, there being eight Gibbes, as well as eight other children, the oldest of whom was fifteen. Once dressed, Mr. Gibbes was placed in his rolling chair and taken into the spacious front hall to join the others.

The British had no inkling that any one was up until they heard the rolling of Mr. Gibbes's heavy chair toward the front door. Thinking that the rolling sound was a cannon, the troops fixed bayonets and prepared to rush in when the signal for assault was given. They were startled and drew back when the door was suddenly flung open and they beheld the stately figure of the invalid Mr. Gibbes surrounded by numerous well-dressed women and children. The effect was so unexpected that the soldiers involuntarily presented arms as a sign of respect.

Mr. Gibbes addressed the intruders courteously, and the officers took immediate possession of the house. Setting an example for the others, Mrs. Gibbes showed not a hint of fear, causing all her charges to be treated with the respect that aristocrats expected from their peers. At the dinner table she was remarkably gracious to her uninvited guests, and the enemy officers, being gentlemen themselves, involuntarily responded to her hospitality.

But while the family entertained the officers in the big house, the soldiers were busy helping themselves to whatever they chose to take on the plantation grounds. They were boisterous and unruly after they broke into the wine room, drank to intoxication and carried off the servants. Most of the family plate was saved only because a faithful slave secretly buried it just in the nick of time.

When news of the British encampment reached Charles Town, two galleys of colonial troops were sent out. It was dark when they arrived. They disembarked and started shooting their muskets at the drunken British soldiers.

Unknown to Mr. Gibbes, the rescuers had been given strict instructions not to fire upon the house for fear of injuring the family. Although the enemy had stolen all of their horses, Gibbes advised his household to flee the mayhem. The refugee group set out on foot for the safety of a nearby plantation, all the while pushing Mr. Gibbes's chair on wheels across the uneven ground as they trudged through the darkness in a cold, soaking rain.

Meanwhile, seeking to avoid hitting the mansion house, the rescuers shot in the direction of the evacuees, whom they could not see in the darkness. Their shots cut the bushes and struck trees on every side of the little group. The servants were terrified.

To appreciate their condition, one must consider the clothes of the day. Women of the upper classes wore tightly laced bodices, long skirts, flimsy shoes and hair coifed high upon the head. Men wore knee britches, high stockings, buckled shoes, vests and sometimes wigs. The going must have been extremely difficult.

By the time the group reached the houses of some of the plantation laborers, Mrs. Gibbes was so exhausted by the responsibilities that had fallen upon her shoulders that she wrapped herself in a blanket and collapsed onto one of the slave's beds. Others in the company must have been equally exhausted from their exertions.

Once it was safe to regroup, a headcount was taken. It was discovered that, in the haste of the evacuation, little John Fenwick had been left behind. The slaves utterly refused to go back amidst the falling lead, and Mr. Gibbes did not feel that he could trust them while the roar of the distant guns could still be heard breaking the silence of the night.

Young Mary Anna Gibbes, the oldest daughter in the family, volunteered to rescue the child. Although only thirteen, she braved the chilling rain, darkness and dangers to return to the house a full mile distant. Once there, she had to overcome the objections of the British sentinel, using both entreaties and tears until he finally let her enter. Mary Anna found the child sleeping upstairs on the third floor. The courageous young girl took

Fenwick Hall seen before it was restored in the 1930s. John's Island suffered a devastating fire in the 1860s, and plantation houses that survived fell into disrepair. (Peaceful Retreat did not fare as well as its neighbor.) *Courtesy the Charleston Museum, Charleston, South Carolina.*

him in her arms and, amid the shot and shell, returned to her anxious family. The child she rescued was John Roger Fenwick, a cousin who later became a lieutenant colonel who fought with distinction in the War of 1812.

Today, all that remains of Pleasant Retreat is a 1797 watercolor by Charles Fraser and anecdotes about the brave young heroine, Mary Anna Gibbes.

Nearby Fenwick Place has seen the vicissitudes of war, Reconstruction and the demise of the Sea Island cotton industry. The house has survived and is now surrounded by the development that is gradually destroying what was left of the rural Sea Island culture.

SHIPWRECKED

After the War of 1812, the United States government began to protect its ports in earnest, and in the 1820s the U.S. Army Corps of Engineers began to build defensive fortifications around Charleston's harbor. They started with Fort Moultrie and Fort Johnson and quickly expanded their program to the construction of Fort Sumter and an erosion control system on Sullivan's Island.

An English engineer and officer in the British Merchant Marine named Philip Francis Middleton was one of the men who came to work on this mammoth construction project. He worked on the jetties designed to keep the shore near Fort Moultrie from being washed into the sea. These jetties were always referred to as groins, and their sand-covered remains can still be seen near the old fort.

Middleton did well, married, had children and returned to his native land after his wife died. He named his oldest son Charles Francis, although everyone called him Charlie. Young Charlie Middleton was trained to be an engineer, like his father before him, and there was a great demand for those skills in antebellum rice cultivation.

The South Carolina rice industry was located primarily in the low-lying coastal areas where the crops could be irrigated by the ebb and flow of the tides. The plantations around Georgetown were the major rice producers, and by 1840 the Georgetown area grew almost half of the rice in the United States. The engineering skill and manpower required to construct and maintain an

Shipwrecked blockade runner off the coast of Sullivan's Island. (Groins in foreground.) *Courtesy Library of Congress.*

integrated irrigation system were enormous. It involved "miles of levees, ditches, and culverts, interspersed with assorted floodgates, trunks, and drains." It was a highly labor-intensive industry that utilized not only slave labor, but also the inanimate power provided by "water, wind and steam."[38]

There were endless opportunities for a skilled engineer in the 1850s, when Charlie Middleton courted Augusta Loftus Jordan. Charlie called her "Gus" or "Gusta," and like many South Carolinians, she had an interesting background. Gusta Jordan was a descendant of French Protestants (Huguenots), who had immigrated to Dublin some time after the revocation of the Edict of Nantes.

Louis XIV's revocation of the Edict of Nantes had had enormous consequences. In 1598, Henry IV had issued an edict giving French Protestants sanctuary cities and civil rights, in the hope that it would unite the country after almost a century of religious wars. The most infamous incident was the St. Bartholomew's Day massacre in 1572. Almost ninety years later, Louis XIV revoked the edict in an attempt to intimidate Protestants into converting to Catholicism. Fearing persecution, Protestants left France, taking with them skills in silk production, glass making, silversmithing and cabinet making. This "brain drain" practically eliminated the French middle class and is considered to have been one of the precipitating factors of the French Revolution.

Things certainly must have been very unpleasant for French Protestants in Dublin. Several Protestant Jordans, including Gusta's father, were hanged in effigy, resulting in her lifelong aversion to Irish Roman Catholics. When the family received a legacy of fine plantation land in Beaufort, South Carolina, bequeathed with the stipulation that the entire Jordan family claim it in person, they did. And so it was that thirty Jordan beneficiaries arrived in Charleston and attended St. Michael's Church, taking up all the front pews of the north gallery. Sometime thereafter they went to Beaufort to receive their inheritance.

Charleston customs were quaint back then. As a large group of young people walked along the high battery, Charlie and Gusta would contrive to lag behind the others as they courted. According to the affectionate tone in Charlie's letters while he was a blockade runner, it was evidently a love match. They were married in St. Peter's Church on Logan Street, a handsome building that was destroyed by the fire of 1861. (In the 1970s, contractor Waveland Fitzsimons built a six-unit condominium on the church site and was thought to have moved several graves to the southern portion of the lot. Number 10 Logan was one of the first condominiums in the city. The noted local historian Jonathan Poston and three members of the Middleton family have lived there.)

The newlywed couple moved to Georgetown, where Charlie worked on the plantation of a Mr. Tucker. They had three children, two of whom survived to adulthood. Things went well for the growing family until their lives were shattered by the onset of the Civil War.

After the hostilities started, Captain C.F. Middleton participated in the defense of Sullivan's Island and later became an engineer on two Confederate blockade runners, the *Mary Celestia* and the *Lelia*. Both vessels were owned by Crenshaw and Company, a Southern firm that provided supplies to the Confederate forces. The *Mary Celestia* and the *Lelia* were both built in England on the Mersey River in the Liverpool shipyard of William C. Miller and Sons.

Running the blockade attracted a special group of men—men not only drawn to the enormous potential profits, but men who were also willing to risk the dangers of eluding the union ships that blockaded the Southern seaports. The exploits of some blockade runners, like the fictitious Rhett Butler, have become legendary. Others met bankruptcy, shipwreck and death through a variety of circumstances. With abundant expendable funds, blockade runners had a reputation for riotous living, practicing that old maxim "eat, drink, and be merry, for tomorrow we die." There were also many responsible, lonesome family men who felt it their duty to serve their homeland, their beloved Dixie. Engineer Charlie Middleton was one of them.

It is uncertain exactly when Middleton joined Crenshaw and Company, for his surviving letters to his wife start in April 1864. He was then thirty-three years old. His letters indicate that he did not engage in the transatlantic crossings, but rather served on boats being run from Wilmington, North Carolina, to Nassau and Bermuda. His letters also suggest that while the boats were being outfitted in Southern ports, the crew was sometimes able to visit their homes.

In July 1864, Middleton was serving aboard the *Mary Celestia*, a fast, side-wheel steamer weighing 207 tons. It is unknown how many successful crossings the ship actually made, for it had taken numerous aliases to confuse the Yankees, including the *Bijou* and

Marie Celeste.[39] What is known about the *Mary Celestia* is that, while en route from Wilmington to Bermuda, the boat was discovered by a blockader. Poor visibility in a driving rain prevented the crew from seeing their pursuer until it was bearing down upon them. The seas were rough and the *Mary Celestia* was heavy laden with cotton. According to an eyewitness account:

> *Had a most exciting chase by a vessel equally as fast as ourselves. We were chased from six in the morning until 2 in the evening, and we lightened our ship by throwing overboard some 100 Bales of King cotton. When our pursuer, seeing the chances of getting our ship and the balance of the cotton so very poor turned around to pick up what had been thrown overboard, and I think he must have had a fine time at it, for we cut the bands of most of the bales, and then you know it was all in loose mass of bulk floating on the sea…I suppose the* Mary Celestia *sooner or later will be captured but I hope and trust in God I will not be in her.*[40]

After the Bermuda adventure, the *Mary Celestia* headed for Nassau. While in port, Middleton amused himself as best he could, and the ship took on a cargo of arms and munitions consigned to the Confederate forces in Richmond.

The *Mary Celestia* had not been at sea for more than twenty-fours when yellow fever broke out. This was not unusual, for during the summer of 1864 this dreaded disease, called "yellow Jack," took many lives both on land and at sea. (Not knowing that the disease was mosquito-borne, people attempted to contain it through isolation and fumigation.)

The Cape Fear pilot, John William (Billy) Anderson, was stricken shortly after the ship left port. He refused the captain's offer to return to Nassau, saying that "he would rest when they reached home." By the second day at sea, Anderson was delirious. This placed the ship in jeopardy, as he was the only pilot on board who was familiar with the treacherous New Inlet bar.

Charles Francis Middleton, taken in Bermuda while he was running the blockade. *Courtesy Middleton family.*

As the *Mary Celestia* neared the North Carolina coast, it was spotted at dawn by a blockader in the Union fleet. Union shells passed through the rigging and sent up columns of spray as the Yankee boat chased the *Mary Celestia* toward the dangerous inlet. Hearing the commotion, the dying John Billy Anderson insisted that he be taken to the bridge to guide the vessel as it raced for the protective guns of Fort Fisher. Two seamen helped the courageous man walk to the wheelhouse and propped him up as he guided the vessel across the bar. With the harbor in sight, Anderson suddenly coughed up black vomit, a sure sign of death from yellow fever, and died almost immediately thereafter.[41] It was a heroic act long remembered, especially by Charlie Middleton, for his dear friend John Billy had given him a gold watch and chain, a keepsake still in the possession of Middleton's descendants.

When the *Mary Celestia* arrived in Wilmington, instead of receiving a hero's welcome, along with eight other vessels, it was quarantined for over a month because of the yellow fever epidemic.

The tedium of being confined to the steamer was difficult for the men, and Middleton wrote of the loneliness, boredom and privations of not being allowed ashore. The isolated men were forced to go up the beach, where barrels of fresh water were left for their use. Although the men were obliged to wash their own clothes and wear them rough-dry, their greatest privation was the lack of letters from home.

As it turned out, in spite of attempted bribery, the men were never permitted to disembark in Wilmington, and Middleton's letters home put up a brave front during those wasted weeks. He had evidently lost all enthusiasm for blockade running, and only a sense of loyalty to the Confederacy and Mr. Crenshaw's assurances of a better ship kept him from resigning from his employment.

Before departing on another Bermuda run, Middleton deposited John Billy Anderson's treasured gift, a breastpin and a belt containing $600 worth of gold coins with his employer in Wilmington as a precaution in the event of capture.

On September 6, 1864, the *Mary Celestia* left on what became its final voyage to Bermuda. As described by Dave Horner in *The Blockade Runners*,

> *The fast little ship made a quick run through the East End channels and was cruising at thirteen knots along the South shore. About 6:00 p.m. she eased toward land to permit her owner, Colonel Crenshaw, and pilot Virgin to leave the vessel in the vicinity of Gibb's Hill Light House. After a few minutes, First Officer Stuart called the pilot's attention to some breakers ahead, to which it seems Mr. Virgin replied, "I know every rock about here as well as I know my own house." And the pilot refused to take heed to the warning. Seeing the obvious danger, the first mate ordered the helm put hard over. But it was too late. His command had hardly been acknowledged*

when the Mary Celeste *struck the reef. She sank in six to eight minutes.*[42]

The only life lost was that of the chief cook, who went below to get a prized possession. The door slammed shut on the sinking vessel, taking him down with it. The Confederate authorities demanded an explanation of how a boat could hit a reef in smooth water in broad daylight. They claimed that the pilot had been bribed by the U.S. consul to Bermuda. Although the shipwreck was investigated, it was soon forgotten in the midst of the necessities of war. Memories of the sinking have been preserved in the ballad, "The Wreck of the *Mary Celeste*."

As for the shipwrecked mariners, with yellow fever raging in Bermuda, they were again quarantined. This time many of them died, causing great sorrow for those left behind. Middleton fared better than most and lived comfortably in the country with the ship's chief mate and the kindly captain, Arthur Sinclair, a commander in the Confederate navy.

Arthur Sinclair was from a distinguished naval family and had served under his father during Matthew C. Perry's voyage to Japan. Once hostilities began, Sinclair resigned his commission in the U.S. Navy and served on numerous Confederate ships. He was promoted to the rank of commander after his ship, the *Squib*, successfully exploded a primitive torpedo against the USS *Minnesota*. He was assigned to the *Mary Celestia* in July 1864.

Middleton described Sinclair as "a real fatherly old man and says we are his children, and is always lecturing us if we go in the sun or night air and I think he thinks a great deal of me."[43]

While "yellow jack" ran its course in Southern ports, the blockade was tightening, and no ships had come into Bermuda after the sinking of the *Mary Celestia*. Middleton's letters from Bermuda indicate how the changing fortunes of the war had persuaded him to return home for good. He determined to take the first boat bound for a Southern port, for the blockade was tightening its stranglehold.

To escape Bermuda before yellow fever claimed their lives, Arthur Sinclair persuaded Middleton to join him on the maiden voyage of the *Lelia*, a blockade runner then under construction in Liverpool. The two men booked passage out of Bermuda on a mail ship and proceeded on to England.

Because of the political intrigues of the times, Arthur Sinclair was registered as a passenger on *Lelia*, not as a Confederate officer. He was slated to take command when the ship reached Bermuda. To honor the distinguished captain, Crenshaw had named his prize vessel *Lelia*, after Sinclair's wife. Before leaving port, Crenshaw presented Sinclair with a gold watch and chain complete with a compass and locket containing a lock of Lelia Sinclair's hair.

Charlie Middleton's last letter home was written from Liverpool on December 16, 1864. He again expressed his concerns about being so far from home as the news of Sherman's exploits trickled in. The closing blessing to his family is pathetically poignant, for his "fine ship" went down less than a month later off the coast of Llandudno, Wales.

It was a classic tragedy. In January 1865 northwesterly gales had been battering the west coast of England for a week. Although the barometer was ominously low, no storm warning had yet been hoisted as the *Lelia* left Liverpool on that fateful Friday the thirteenth. Lulled into a false sense of security, the vessel proceeded down the Mersey River and dropped anchor to prepare for the voyage to Bermuda.

The *Lelia* was a large ironclad vessel of 640 tons equipped with powerful English steam engines. The ship was heavy laden and low in the water. As the ship left the sheltered waters of the Mersey, the wind picked up and the *Lelia* suddenly encountered the full force of a fierce winter storm. The vessel pitched and rolled as waves unrelentingly crashed onto the deck.

Unprepared for the heavy seas, Captain Thomas Buxton Skinner ordered that the vessel be slowed and the anchors hoisted aboard. A huge wave lifted one of the anchors and smashed the fluke through the deck. Another wave washed away the iron covering of a scuttle and the water began pouring into the *Lelia*'s bow.

Through a series of mishaps, the crew could not access the equipment necessary to pump out the vessel and the deck of the ship soon sank to the level of the raging sea, causing the frail structure of the steel hull to fall below the waterline. As described by Francis B.C. Bradlee in *Blockade Running During the Civil War*, the powerful engines "almost forced the framework through the delicate steel shell, causing it to buckle and crumple and give way from the rivets, against the mighty pressure of the waves."[44]

Once it became obvious that the *Lelia* could not be saved, Captain Skinner gave orders to abandon ship. As the bow began sinking, all of the men crowded on the stern where the lifeboats were stored. Of the four lifeboats, two got tangled in the rigging and were useless before they could be lowered into the water. The crew and passengers who managed to get into the remaining lifeboats met catastrophe when both boats capsized in the rough seas before reaching the Mersey River lightship. Only twelve freezing and exhausted men were pulled out of the sea and returned safely to Liverpool. A rescue effort manned by the Liverpool lifeboats also met calamity, and seven men who had refused to don their cumbersome life jackets drowned when their boat capsized in the storm-tossed waters.

True to the tradition of the sea, the brave Captain Skinner went down with his ship in spite of the fact that he had had an opportunity to board the last lifeboat that made it to the water. His last act was to fire up distress rockets from the ill-fated ship. In all, the disaster took the lives of fifty men. One of those unfortunates was Charles Francis Middleton.

Although many ships went down off the English coast during that January storm, the sensational wreck of the *Lelia* received the most attention. The shipwreck was thoroughly investigated by the Board of Trade in Liverpool, but in time, the incident faded from the news; that is, until what remained of a man, still fully dressed

Union soldiers relax after Fort Fisher fell in January 1865. *Courtesy Library of Congress.*

in his overcoat and uniform, was pulled from the sea four months later. He was positively identified as Captain Sinclair because of Crenshaw's parting gift, the ornate gold watch, which was still in his pocket. The watch had stopped at 4:10 p.m., marking the time when Arthur Sinclair was thrown into the sea from the lifeboat that had overturned before it could clear the sinking ship.

Fort Fisher fell in January 1865, and in time, Gusta Middleton realized that her husband wasn't coming back. During the harsh time of Reconstruction, she struggled to support her family by opening a millinery shop at 130 King Street using her last asset, the $600 in gold left in Wilmington by her husband. Her brother-in-law William strongly disapproved of having a lady "in the trade," and when he could not dissuade her, he did not speak to her for many years.

It was unfortunate that Charleston ladies were so impoverished that the enterprising millinery venture failed. The bereaved

Middleton family scraped by and somehow eked out a living by selling miscellany and homemade hats in the little shop. They were so financially strapped that Gusta could not afford to buy a bucket and had to dip a set of porcelain pitchers into their cistern to provide the household with water. The pitchers were decorated with her husband's initials painted in gold on their sides. One has survived and is a cherished heirloom now owned by a great-grandson, also named Charles Francis. Charlie Middleton's letters were lovingly preserved with the notation "Sacred treasures" in Augusta Middleton's hand on the back.

As the sinking of both the *Mary Celestia* and the *Lelia* occurred off English waters, those faraway shipwrecks have not been incorporated into local Charleston lore. Charles Francis Middleton's letters, now in the possession of the Charleston Historical Society, provide a personal view of the blockade and how it affected several South Carolina families. The letters were published in the *Bermuda Quarterly* in 1971.

When Philip Francis Middleton arrived in South Carolina, there was a rigid social hierarchy; rice planters were considered the most prestigious of the plantation families, followed by the sea-island cotton planters and inland cotton growers. The descendants of Arthur and Edward Middleton, who had emigrated from Barbados in the late seventeenth century, had been part of the plantation aristocracy long before the Revolution. According to family tradition, Philip Francis Middleton was approached by a member of the established Middleton family who requested that he change the spelling of his name to "Myddleton" in order to distinguish his surname from that of "the Middleton Family."

HIGH COTTON

Ten Limehouse Street

After the Civil War ended, the families of those who fought for the Confederacy were reduced to unimaginably dire circumstances. The land had been ravaged by war and was occupied by soldiers once the Union invaded the South. Worse yet, because South Carolina had started the war, many Northern politicians in Congress wanted revenge. It was a desperate situation. As described by Charleston's farsighted Episcopal minister the Reverend A. Toomer Porter:

> *The entire wealth of the state had been swept away... The mere youth, the seed corn, as Mrs. Jefferson Davis called them, had been taken into the army, and for four years had not been at school... The railroads had been destroyed, banks had failed, factories we had none; insurance companies had all failed. There was, therefore, no source of income and the most calamitous result was the inability to educate our children... Unhappy is the land which has no educated, cultured class. If everything is on a low, dead level, then ignorance and deterioration are inevitable.*[45]

In 1866, Dr. Porter went to Boston and New York as an emissary of the South Carolina Episcopal Church to raise funds for a theological seminary and a school in which to educate the freed black children. An eloquent spokesman, he returned to

Charleston not only with generous contributions from Northern Episcopalians, but also as a trustee for the Marine Hospital. It had been condemned by the federal government and was sold in trust for a colored school with the blessing of President Johnson himself. As one of the trustees, Porter returned and converted the Marine Hospital into a school for the children of former slaves. (In 1895, the building was taken over by a black Baptist preacher who turned it into an orphanage. Located on Franklin Street, the hospital was designed by Robert Mills. This handsome Gothic Revival structure had originally been built for sick and disabled merchant seamen.)

However, the white children still had no educational facilities whatsoever. This situation was about to change. On October 25, 1867, Porter had an experience that altered the direction of his life. According to his autobiography, he was kneeling at the grave of his son Toomer at Magnolia Cemetery, when suddenly a voice commanded, "Stop grieving for the dead and do something for the living."

Startled, Porter looked around and saw no one. The voice continued, "Your child is enjoying what you only hope for; but see his young companions who are mostly poor orphans without schools and churches. Take them and educate them."

Thus inspired, Porter returned home and shared his experience with his invalid wife, who immediately offered to give up the income from her dowry to support the effort. Once again Porter traveled north to raise money. Within two months of his life-changing experience, Porter again returned, this time with sufficient funds to open a new school for impoverished white children. Porter's school opened shortly thereafter, taking in 550 pupils, 125 of them girls. His students were from once-prosperous families who understood the value of an education.

Fatherless Charles Francis Middleton Jr. was one of the fortunate Charleston boys who attended Dr. Porter's school, and he was one of Porter's many success stories. Born on August 15, 1859, he grew to manhood during the painful Reconstruction years.

Middleton's father had been a blockade runner who drowned when his vessel sank off the coast of Wales in January 1865. Like many other Southern boys of his generation, Charles Middleton was obliged to take on heavy responsibilities early in life. He began his business career at the age of fifteen, when he finished Dr. Porter's school. He wrote a polished letter, which landed him his first job as office boy. It was a simple letter that read:

> *Dear Sir,*
>
> *Having seen advertisement in paper, I thought that I would apply for the situation. Having gone through Rev. A. T. Porter's school I feel confident that I could fill the vacancy. Last year during the two months of vacation I was with Mr. Julius A. Blake in East Bay below the Post Office. I am very anxious to get into business, but there being no openings and so many boys wanting situations that I had almost despaired of getting a place this month.*
>
> *It has always been my desire to get into a firm, with whom I could always remain, and endeavor to raise myself by my own merit and attention to the business.*
>
> *If this, my application, meets with your approval, address*
> *Charles F. Middleton*
> *130 King Street.*

Charm, intelligence and diligence helped the young man support his mother, her sister and his younger brother. They were so poor and food was so scarce that Middleton chewed tobacco instead of taking lunch to work, a habit that he had developed as an appetite suppressant while still at Dr. Porter's school.

By the time he was twenty-four, Middleton had done so well that he decided to take a wife. He courted Miss Lucile Johnson, who was staying on the upper end of Sullivan's Island. One fateful day, fully intending to propose marriage, he took the ferry from Charleston to Mount Pleasant.

As the "muley car" bore him across the causeway toward the island, the would-be suitor impulsively decided to visit some friends along the way. He got off the trolley at Grandma Walter's boardinghouse and there he beheld her niece, young Lois Hazlehurst. She was beautiful, with red-gold hair, finely chiseled features and smooth white skin. Mr. Middleton was smitten and later told his family that when he beheld her shabby shoes, he longed to present her with a new pair.

Miss Lucile was promptly forgotten as another, more interesting courtship was begun. Lois Hazlehurst and Charles Middleton were married in the little Episcopal Church on Sullivan's Island. She was barely sixteen.

It was four years before their first child, Hazel, was born. They had twelve children, eight of whom lived. Theirs was a happy marriage.

Cotton made many a fortune in the antebellum South, and even after "the War," the cotton business continued to be very profitable until the boll weevil took its toll. Charles Francis Middleton Jr. was one of the entrepreneurs who made his way in the cotton business. At the time of his marriage, he was working in naval stores, which supplied the navy with turpentine and tar. Later he learned the intricacies of the cotton business while a junior clerk for A.J. Salinas, a cotton factor on Vendue Range. (Factors financed the famers' crops.)

Exporting cotton required an understanding of worldwide markets and finding reliable sources of cotton to purchase, compact and ship. At the urging of his wife, Middleton went into business for himself. He was the senior partner of Middleton & Ravenel with W.B. Ravenel. They separated after a time, and in 1908 he founded Middleton & Company, an enterprise that exported many thousands of bales.

Middleton also established the Concentration Compress and Warehouse Company in 1914, which by 1920 was described by the *Charleston News & Courier* as the largest in the city, with a storage capacity of twenty thousand bales. At the time of

Lois Hazlehurst and Charles Francis Middleton, taken a few years after their marriage. *Courtesy Middleton family.*

his death in 1939, Middleton was the oldest member of the Charleston Cotton Exchange.

Middleton & Company business offices were located in an unassuming brick building at the corner of Hasell and Concord Streets. Across the street, on the Cooper River, was a warehouse.

Concentration Compress and Warehouse, circa 1915. *Courtesy Middleton family.*

The front parlor of 10 Limehouse Street. *Courtesy Middleton family.*

Locomotives backed freight cars onto the rail siding, where the ginned cotton was unloaded by teams of stevedores who sang or cussed in their rich bass voices while they worked. A huge steam press shaped the cotton into bales. Once banded and labeled, the bales were loaded onto the cargo ships that docked at the bustling wharf.

When the company began to prosper, Middleton purchased a home large enough to accommodate his growing family. Lois Middleton had set her sights on the handsome brick, Federal-style house at 21 Legare Street. She told her family that she cried with disappointment when her husband surprised her with the keys to 10 Limehouse, even though it was one of the two most imposing residences on the block.

Number 10 Limehouse was a large and comfortable three-story house that stretched from the street to Greenhill Alley. There were lots of stairs and lots of rooms. In time the family discovered that, with so many children and so many flights of stairs, their household had been "read out" in Negro churches (their way of blacklisting employers.)

In flush times, the Middletons lived well. One day Mr. Middleton had a windfall at the Cotton Exchange and brought home several gold pieces, which he tossed into his wife's lap. One fell onto the floor and rolled beneath a heavy piece of furniture, where it was left because of the difficulty in retrieving it. The next day the cotton market plummeted. Dressed in the formal Victorian attire of a stiff, starched collar and a corset for the lady, the young couple laughed uproariously as they searched on their hands and knees for the missing gold piece.

Although the family may have looked rich to outsiders, they were always frugal, as the hard times of Reconstruction had the same tempering effect that the Great Depression would have seventy years later. The family worried about taxes and the market throughout the course of the enterprise. And it seemed as if the Middleton men were always reminding their wives about frugality.

The façade of the Middleton office building located at 231 East Bay. *Courtesy Middleton family.*

Middleton & Company had its woes. It opened an office in Savannah with the bookkeeper, Edward T. Trenholm, in charge. When the business failed, Middleton had to personally go to Savannah to discharge the bank debts. After the Savannah debacle, Middleton decided to export cotton to Europe, where he traveled many times in the ensuing years. His son, Abbott Middleton, moved his family to Dallas and opened a branch office there. A clerk stole a large sum, and once again the senior Middleton had to help shut down the concern.

All in all, the company prospered until the disastrous Belzone cotton affair. The senior Middleton had just lost his beloved wife, and to get his mind on more pleasant things, his oldest son took him on a business trip to Europe. While they were gone, a boat loaded with cotton sank somewhere near New Orleans, and the cotton was offered at a ridiculously low price. It was a speculative purchase and had to be snapped up quickly. Abbot Middleton and A. Pringle discussed the purchase and decided to buy. The interior cotton proved to be a soggy mess, and the Middletons "lost their shirts" as they put it. As a result, the family had an early entry into the economic vicissitudes associated with the Great Depression.

Willoughby, Charles and Hazel Middleton. *Courtesy Middleton family.*

It was only through the income generated from thirty thousand bales of "government cotton" stored at the Concord Street warehouse for a penny a day for each bale that the Middleton families were carried through the thirties. The cotton business was still sluggish when the Second World War began. Young Charlie Middleton tried to preserve the wharf before he joined the Marine Corps. After his cousin Abbott joined the U.S. Naval Air Force in 1941 and Charlie's untimely death a few years later, the elder Middleton brothers sold the company to Cheshire Sullivan in 1944.[46]

Charles Middleton's business successes and personal charisma earned for him a coveted invitation to the St. Cecilia Society. Only a very few lucky latecomers have been invited to join the descendants of the aristocratic old families. Originally a music society, the St. Cecilia is among the most exclusive organizations in the world. Some young eligibles have had to wait for a member to die before they were admitted.

Attending the St. Cecilia was so important that there is a delightful anecdote about a conversation at a funeral. As the story goes, a member of a bereaved family lamented,

> *George never could get into St. Cecilia. I have been thinking that now that he has gone, probably his brother can take George's daughter to the Ball. And if Eleanor can go to the St. Cecilia, I'm sure that George would have been glad to die.*

No young lady could be a debutante unless she was presented by her parents at the St. Cecilia. At the balls, no gentleman smoked, and only sherry was served on the dance floor. Debutantes sat with their chaperones, and no lady was permitted to leave the floor until the glittering assemblage descended from the ballroom in a grand cotillion, led by the president and the Bride of the Ball. The lavish supper was followed by more card dances.

When their older daughter had her "coming out," the Middletons had a large reception at their home on January 10, 1911. Preparations went on for days, and Mrs. Middleton delivered the invitations personally, hiring a hack on January 5. The day before the big event, a protective canvas was put up and decorative greens were festooned around stair rails and doorways. As with functions of later years, "crockery" was hired for the occasion. The reception was reputed to have been a great success.

At another debutante party at 10 Limehouse, the huge mahogany folding doors between the dining room and the library were pushed back, providing a tremendous dancing area next to the dining room. The entire downstairs was decorated with smilax, gorgeous flowers and colorful balloons. The orchestra played in the hall, and hot supper was served at midnight. Although the party was given during Prohibition, champagne was served, as Mr. Middleton was great friends with many ship captains who were delighted to share their effervescent spirits with someone who had entertained them frequently.

Once his children were married, Charles Middleton gave each of them a home. After that, the aging Mr. Middleton refused to spend any further money refurbishing 10 Limehouse. They rented the almost empty house that Lois Middleton had never wanted and moved in with their oldest child, Hazel Baker, at 54 King Street. Number 10 Limehouse Street was sold just before Lois Middleton died in 1927.

After his wife's death, the senior Middleton moved in with his oldest son, Charlie, at 24 New Street. Although he was pursued by some of Charleston's most aristocratic elderly ladies, he never remarried. He lived a full life and died at home in 1939 at age eighty. His personality was so dominant that to this day his wit and humor are remembered by those who were fortunate enough to have known him.

CHANGE IN FAMILY FORTUNES

One Pitt Street

Number 1 Pitt Street is a house with a history that is almost as interesting as its inhabitants. Unfortunately, as you walk by today, there is no historical marker to advise passersby about the house or its occupants. Harleston Village was a fashionable neighborhood when this handsome, two-story brick house was built in 1848, but by the twentieth century Pitt Street was considered uptown (north of Broad), and living there was slightly less socially desirable than living downtown, just a couple of blocks farther south.

Number 1 Pitt Street was built by Charles Henry Lanneau, a descendent of one of the French Catholics whom the British deported from Acadia after the fall of the fort in Louisburg, Nova Scotia, during the French and Indian War. The British dumped French exiles all along the East Coast, and a thousand unfortunates landed in Charleston. The Lanneaus were one of the few French Canadian families that prospered in South Carolina; their descendants built several houses on Pitt Street.

During the Civil War, number 1 Pitt Street was said to have been used to incarcerate Federal soldiers. It survived the devastating earthquake of 1886, in which the tremors were felt as far away as Bermuda and Ontario. (Seismographers compare it to the earthquake that devastated San Francisco in 1906.) The house was repaired after the earthquake and was purchased by William Baynard Simons in 1889.[47]

One Pitt Street after the earthquake of 1886. *Courtesy the Charleston Museum, Charleston, South Carolina.*

In later years, Baynard Simons was a lanky, quiet man, with many resemblances to Abraham Lincoln. He was somewhat remote, but sometimes he would tell his family about his privations as a boy on war-ravaged Edisto Island, a barrier island south of Charleston.

After the Revolution, indigo production declined. Planters on the barrier islands changed crops and prospered by growing the prized Sea Island long-staple cotton. The profits were so great that every inch of arable land was cultivated. Although agriculture was the livelihood, sport hunting and fishing were an integral part of country life. The wealthy planters would vacation in places like Summerville, Rockville, Sullivan's Island or even the mountains of North Carolina. In the winter they came to Charleston to enjoy the frivolities of city life.

A huge population of slaves worked the land and did the domestic labor. They spoke Gullah, a combination of English and African dialects. Some say that Gullah had been developed by the traders in Africa. Many of the children who grew up with black nurses talked much like their Dahs. Most households loved their domestic servants and treated them almost as family.

It was said that visiting Virginia aristocrats were shocked that the Carolina ladies spoke like "Negroes." One of the Edisto stories about Gullah accents was about a young man who came courting the daughters of a wealthy family. The daughters spoke the local dialect, and their mother, fearing that this would scare off the would-be suitor, forbade her daughters from speaking while their guest visited. As the mother entertained the caller, the girls sat primly, doing needlework. All of a sudden one of the girls dropped a spool of thread and surprised the young man by saying,

"Titta, han' me da tread."

To which her sister replied:"Hush up. Ain't ya know Ma tol' ya no' fo' speak?" As the story goes, the suitor left shortly thereafter, never to return.

Edisto typified the Old South sea islands—handsome homes surrounded by massive oak trees with their outstretched branches draped with Spanish moss; large, cultivated cotton fields; and tidal creeks bordered by marsh grasses that changed their colors with the season. It was a lifestyle that completely disappeared after the Union army invaded the South. The plantation system collapsed and poverty set in. All that remained was a love of the rich, dark, sandy soil, the musty smell of the brackish water and the quiet peace—something still in the blood of the descendants of those island inhabitants, both white and black.

It is a good thing that living on the land made people resourceful. During Reconstruction, fatherless Baynard Simons had been obliged to start working at the age of twelve, having the responsibility for his widowed mother and several other dependents. His mother, Susan Caroline Baynard, had grown up at Prospect Hill,[48] and she had been outrageously spoiled. Supposedly, her father would bribe her to behave. She never learned to dress herself. When she could no longer depend upon servants to button her shoes and lace up her clothes, her children were forced to take on the task.

Baynard Simons riding his invention, a rail car that transported fertilizer to the loading docks at Planter's Fertilizer Mill. *Courtesy Middleton family.*

After the war, Baynard pounded brickbats into powder, which he put into matchboxes and peddled to the housewives of Edisto Island for a penny apiece. The moistened dust was used to cover up the black stains on smoke-darkened fireplace surrounds. Food was scarce, and he remembered breakfasts that consisted of but one biscuit for each person.

Later, the family lived in Charleston, and Baynard attended Dr. A. Toomer Porter's school for impoverished boys as one of the famous "seed corn." (The "seed corn" were charity white students who were schooled in the hope that Charleston's future would not be blighted by a leadership deprived of a classical education.) To supplement the meager meals he brought from home, Baynard played tag with the boarders for their breakfasts. Fortunately, he usually won. As fate would have it, he was a friend of his future in-law, Charles F. Middleton Jr.

When he started to court young ladies, Baynard bought a fine green coat with brass buttons. He was such a bumpkin, he said, that he didn't realize that the pushy uptown merchant had sold him a coachman's coat until he heard snickers as he escorted a pretty young girl to the Reverend Porter's Holy Communion Church.

As an adult, Baynard Simons worked for Planter's Fertilizer Mill and became a superintendent. He must have been talented, for he invented an engine that improved the method of transporting fertilizer to the loading docks.

Simons married Laura Adams Hanahan from Columbia and they had six children, two boys and four girls. The first daughter was named Jane Margaret after her great-grandmother, Jane Margaret Scott, who had married James Hopkins Adams in 1832. The Adams-Scott union was said to have joined the two wealthiest families in Richland County, located in the South Carolina midlands.

James Hopkins Adams was educated in the North, having attended prep school in Connecticut and then Yale University.

Susan Caroline Baynard at Prospect Hill, Edisto Island, before the war. *Courtesy Middleton family.*

Family tradition was that he had a very sharp tongue, which he used on his enemies when necessary. He began a political career shortly after his return from college and earned the title of "the Young Nullifier." His career culminated when he was elected governor in 1854. He was one of the three commissioners sent to Washington to decide on the division of government property if South Carolina left the Union.

Adams lost a bid for the U.S. Senate to James Chestnut due to Adams's desire to reopen the slave trade, even then something that was regarded by most of his peers as too radical. (James Chestnut was married to Mary Boykin Chestnut, who is remembered for *A Diary from Dixie*.)

Times have changed and so have attitudes. Adams believed the institution of slavery would ensure the continued prosperity of South Carolina. As governor, he prevented a professor whom he regarded as insufficiently proslavery from becoming president of the South Carolina College, the precursor to the University of South Carolina. He urged the South Carolina Congressional Delegation to attempt to repeal the federal law banning the importation of slaves. He further urged every white family to acquire at least one slave, believing that the surest road to prosperity for South Carolinians was acquiring property, and the best property was human property. To that end, he proposed exempting from taxation the first slave to be purchased, both as a means of encouraging the creation of wealth and to help preserve the institution.

> *To us have been committed the fortunes of this peculiar form of society resulting from the union of unequal races. It has vindicated its claim to the approbation of an enlightened humanity. It has civilized and Christianized the African. It has exalted the white race itself to higher hopes and purposes, and it is perhaps of the most sacred obligation, that we should give it the means of expansion, and that we should press it forward to a perpetuity of progress. The world owes its civilization to slavery. It exists with us in its most desirable and*

enduring form. It is the cornerstone of our republican edifice, and the strongest defense will be found in the education of those entrusted with its preservation.

To be fair, Governor Adams also cared about public education, taxes and agriculture. But slavery was his passion, and the consequences of that passion are the legacy he left. Adams also signed the Ordinance of Secession and had the good sense to die before the war was over, leaving his wife and children to pick up the pieces.

Jane Margaret Scott Adams was a remarkable woman in her own right. By the time of war, she was called "Old Lady," which was regarded as a term of affection and respect for a grandmother.

When Sherman came through Columbia on his infamous march to the sea, the family was warned by a neighboring plantation that the troops were on their way. It was Old Lady who was forced to prepare for and greet the Yankee soldiers.

Tradition has it that a servant helped bury the family silver in a safe place—beside the outhouse. For some reason, the family got up in the middle of the night and reburied the silver, pushing the flatware piece by piece into the ground beside the oak avenue. When the soldiers arrived, the slave rushed out to tell them where the silver was buried. The greedy soldiers dug and dug and dug around that old outhouse. The family retrieved the silver after the soldiers left and found that one fork was missing. Until the day she died, every time she walked along the oak avenue, Old Lady poked around looking for the missing fork.

Not wanting her daughters molested by the invading army, Old Lady had her four unmarried daughters climb through a hole in the ceiling into an unfinished loft. To save their clothing, each person put on as many garments as possible. When the soldiers arrived, the remaining members of the family congregated in the garden outside and watched the soldiers take what they fancied.

That dreadful evening the soldiers danced with young servant girls who had "borrowed" dresses from the daughters' wardrobes.

The party dresses were sneaked back the next morning. Those telltale dresses may have saved the lives of the teenage girls hiding in the loft, for they gave evidence of their presence. As soon as the soldiers had departed, Old Lady retrieved and burned the soiled clothing in disgust.

Although the plantation was ransacked, the family chronicler wrote gratefully that the soldiers did not take the family portraits or books from the extensive library; nor did they mar any furniture. Family tradition is that the house was spared because the union officer had been a school friend of the late Governor Adams and that he tipped his hat to young unseen girls in the attic as he rode away.

Whatever the reason, to their credit, the Union soldiers did not burn the house. What they did destroy was the gin house that contained five hundred bales of cotton. Now that was a terrible loss, for cotton could be sold for a gold dollar a pound in England.

After the war was over, Old Lady ran what was left of the plantation, raising not only her own children, but also caring for relatives and former slaves. Her family was better off than most, for she received a fortune of $100,000 in gold when a hundred bales of cotton got through the Federal blockade early in the war.

In 1865, one of Old Lady's daughters named Laura Keziah married Hobart Doane Hanahan (prounounced "Hanny-han") from Old Dominion plantation on Edisto Island. Mr. Hanahan had been captured by the Yankees, who cut off an infected wounded leg while he was a prisoner. The missing limb was later replaced with a cork leg. At twenty-two years of age, Laura Hanahan died two days after giving birth to a daughter, also named Laura.

The circumstances surrounding Laura Hanahan's death were terrible. She died during a rainy spell and could not be buried in the Episcopal Churchyard at Congaree because the grave would fill up with water. When the interment could not be put off any longer, the coffin was lowered once again and weighted down with heavy stones.

One Pitt Street as it looked when Laura Simons paced the piazza cursing the U.S. government during World War I. *Courtesy Middleton family.*

"Hobie" Hanahan could not care for his infant daughter himself so he left her at Live Oak with her grandmother after his wife's untimely death. He moved to New York, where he made and lost several fortunes in stocks. He visited his child whenever possible and twice a year sent young Laura a barrel of clothes from Lord & Taylor, children's books and candy. Old Lady considered most of the clothes much too fine for country life and would permit Laura to keep only two dresses. The remaining clothes were distributed to impoverished city cousins, who would visit Live Oak wearing Laura's fancy dresses, an injustice she always resented.

Old Lady Adams died at Live Oak in 1885. Because he needed money to buy a home after his marriage, Baynard Simons insisted that Live Oak be sold so that his wife's share could be applied to the purchase of number 1 Pitt Street. Even then, the Simons family had to take in boarders to pay off their mortgage.

Laura Kezia Adams. *Courtesy Middleton family.*

Cash money was so tight during those hard times that a new dress was considered a special event. When the Depression hit in the late 1920s, Margaret Middleton's comment was, "Well, at last this country is getting back to normal."

Live Oak was purchased by a Mr. Hamer for $8,000. The oak avenue eventually disappeared, and the house burned to the ground in 1910. The land was sold to the U.S. government. The site of the old plantation house was near the back south gate of McEntire Air National Guard Base in Richland County.

Laura Hanahan Simons hated Yankees and the Federal government all her life because of her associations with Reconstruction. She wouldn't display the American flag during World War I, and the family feared that she might be arrested

Live Oak burning. *Courtesy Middleton family.*

for sedition because of her numerous, loud, anti-American monologues as she paced back and forth on her Pitt Street "piazza."

After she became a grandmother herself, Laura Simons required the family to call her "Old Lady," in memory of the grandmother who raised her.

THE ODIOUS MR. MACKEY

24 and 26 New Street

New Street is an anomaly in the Charleston street grid. Located just west of Logan Street, it is only one block long, intersecting Broad Street on the diagonal. The irregularity started in the eighteenth century on a small piece of land that jutted out between two tidal creeks south of Broad Street. The land veered out at a slight angle and was called Savage's Green. Because the land was surrounded by marshes and did not lend itself to the rectangular grid of the early town's Grand Modell, it was used for military exercises.

The early colonials enjoyed fancy dress balls, horse racing, music and the performing arts. Charles Town built its first theatre in the 1730s, and by the late eighteenth century the growing town boasted several venues for theatrical performances. In 1792, an elegant theatre, designed to be equal to the first theatres of England, was built on Savage's Green, with a handsome neoclassical façade on Broad Street. The pit entrance was located on what was called at the time Middleton Street, for the Middletons owned much of the land. After the dynamic new theatre was erected at the corner, the street became known as New Theatre Street until a disastrous fire destroyed the building and the block became known simply as New Street.

Although photographs of the times make Charleston look like it was destroyed by Civil War bombardment, in 1861 a disastrous fire destroyed a huge swath of the lower peninsula between the Cooper and Ashley Rivers, including the Broad Street theatre and almost all of the nearby houses, the brick house at 37 New Street being the exception. The desolate area was rebuilt between 1870 and 1890.

Jonathan H. Poston, in his book *The Buildings of Charleston*, describes 24 New Street as the E.A. Mackey House, constructed in 1875. He also says that "three years after the construction of the Mackey House, the machinist Isaac Hayne constructed a similarly styled but smaller-scaled dwelling at 26 New Street."[49] Oral tradition in the Hayne and Middleton families presents a far more intriguing version that revolves around Edmund William McGregor Mackey, the notorious "scalawag" who built both houses.

E.W.M. Mackey was the son of a Charleston physician, Albert Gallatin Mackey, who opposed secession from the Union. During the Confederacy, he was confined within the city limits, where his home was bombarded three times. Judge Thomas Jefferson Mackey, an abolitionist, was his uncle. Against his father's wishes, Mackey's older brother enlisted in the Confederate army and lost part of his hand while holding the flag aloft during a battle.

The younger Mackey was more radical than his brother and had little sympathy for the Southern cause. He was admitted to the bar in 1868, and between 1868 and 1875 he served in the Reconstruction government as sheriff, Charleston alderman and member of the South Carolina General Assembly. He served in the U.S. House of Representatives from the Second District from March 1875 to July 1876. He was reelected to the General Assembly during the hotly contested election of 1876 and again served in the U.S. House of Representatives from May 1882 until his death in 1884.

Mackey was the only prominent "scalawag" to marry a mulatto, Victoria (Vicky) Alice Sumter. She was the great-granddaughter of General Thomas Sumter and was described as "a pretty well-educated octoroon from Sumter County…whom the Sumter family had reared as a ladies maid."[50] They had two sons.

Number 24 New Street, circa
1925. *Courtesy Middleton family.*

According to the deed, in 1873 Mary Pennal sold Mackey a
large double lot on the east side of New Street for the ridiculously
low price of $750, a value that illustrates how depressed the
economy was during Reconstruction. Mackey married in 1874
and commenced to build a fine house for his bride on the north
side of the lot.

As Mackey was away from Charleston for extended periods
while he pursued his political career, he left detailed construction
orders with his builders. Apparently, these instructions were
obeyed to the letter by men who must have enjoyed themselves at
Mackey's expense.

To his horror, Mackey returned to discover that his almost-finished house had no formal staircase to the second floor, only a narrow, dark, back staircase for the servants, which the builders apparently used. When formal stairs were crammed into the narrow entrance hallway, the bottom stair actually touched the front door. The scars of an attempt to remedy the problem are still visible.

Mackey's first house is now known as 26 New Street. According to oral tradition, Mackey abandoned the idea of living there because the improvised hall stairs prevented opening the double front doors wide enough to allow clearance of a casket, it being the custom in those days to view the deceased in the living room. Whatever the reason, Mackey subdivided a generous part of the original lot into the site for another home. The floor plan was similar to, but grander than number 26. It boasted a higher elevation, an impressive entrance hall with a wide staircase leading to an upstairs ballroom, imposing gold leaf mirrors over the mantles, gilt cornices and ornate brass doorknobs. Even the outbuildings behind the house were charming.

Today it may be difficult to understand how the staircase fiasco at 26 New Street could have occurred, but Mr. Mackey's character made it very plausible indeed during the turbulent Reconstruction era, for it has taken a long time for the wounds of the Civil War and Reconstruction to heal. A hundred years later, people still talked about the "damn Yankee" carpetbaggers who came down and stole or taxed away everything they could get their hands on. The defeated Southerners despised their contemporaries who collaborated with them. These "traitors" were contemptuously called "scalawags."

After the war, South Carolina was known as "the prostrate state." People in other parts of the country hated South Carolina for starting the disastrous civil conflict. South Carolina was ruled by a vindictive and corrupt Republican Reconstruction government that was backed by occupying Union troops. The elected officials took full advantage of their new positions. Men who had fought in the Confederacy were prohibited from holding public office.

Pigeon house in the rear yard of 24 New Street (later demolished). *Courtesy Middleton family.*

The once-flourishing economy was in shambles. Dishonest use of public money and patronage were rampant. One of the first acts of the Reconstruction state legislature was to order several thousand dollars worth of gold spittoons. Profligate spending had depleted the state treasury to the extent that there was no money left to cover routine operating expenses—eventually, even the gas lighting at the state capitol had been shut off due to delinquent payments. It all came to a head in the election of 1876.

The centennial election was one of the most acrimonious elections in United States history. The Grant administration had been tarnished by scandals, and the Republicans were in trouble nationally. Due to the hard times after the Panic of 1873, Republicans had already lost their majority in the House. The Republicans needed every electoral vote they could garner to elect their candidate for president, Rutherford B. Hayes. Through a strange twist of fate, South Carolina became the national battleground for the presidency.

The South Carolina gubernatorial candidates were the charismatic former Confederate general Wade Hampton, who had been drafted by the Democrats only two months before the election, and the Republican incumbent from Massachusetts, Daniel Henry Chamberlain. Chamberlain was generally regarded as a thief, but he was well educated and enjoyed a national reputation for decency.

The months before the election saw a frenzied but orderly swell of support for Hampton. His followers adopted a red flannel shirt as their uniform. (In the slang of that day, waving a bloody shirt meant attempting to arouse sectional prejudice. To Hampton's followers, the red shirt symbolized derision of Rutherford Hayes's candidacy.)

Hampton made a triumphal sweep across the state, receiving fanfare that had never been seen before or since. With a backdrop of cannon salutes, flowers and arches across the streets, red-shirted riders by the hundreds and crowds into the thousands cheered Hampton at almost every place he visited.

South Carolina's black voters outnumbered the whites by over thirty thousand. Although five hundred black Democrats rode in the procession that followed Hampton's opening speech in Abbeville, most of the new voters were illiterate Republicans. The few black Democrats were shunned, read out of churches, beaten, denied sexual consortium and even murdered by their own people.

Whenever the "colored Democrats" participated in political activities, they had to be protected by the "Red Shirts." Rioting broke out in Charleston when a group of white men sought to protect black Democrats who were being threatened by armed Hunkidories and Live Oaks, the Republican black factions. After a terrifying march of several blocks up King Street, the endangered Democrats were delivered to the protection of the United States army at the Old Citadel. Mobs of angry blacks then took possession of the streets, attacking whites and smashing store windows.

The Grant administration and Governor Chamberlain tried to stem the Hampton tide. The Republican tactic was to incite the whites so that there would be provocation to summon additional Union troops to maintain order. They tried every trick in the book. Ruthless men told hands working in the rice fields that they would be re-enslaved if the Democrats won. In Charleston, the federal government secretly sent in Enfield rifles to arm their black supporters. Some of the more radical country blacks advocated burning down barns and houses. Responding to false inflammatory reports by partisan Northern newspapers who hated the South, Grant sent in additional federal troops after one upstate disturbance.

The irrepressible E.W.M. Mackey was in the thick of things. His infamous speech attacking Hampton's character at a Beaufort Republican rally was the only one of its type on record during the entire bitter campaign. In spite of his aggressive support for the Republicans, Mackey was denied his request for the lucrative plum on the ballot, Charleston clerk of the court, and was put on the legislative ticket instead. This had long-range consequences.

Election day was November 7. Nationally, Democrat Samuel J. Tilden won the presidential election by a popular vote of 250,000. In the Electoral College count, Tilden had 184 electoral votes, one short of a majority, while Hayes had 165 votes. Twenty electoral votes that would have given Hayes the presidency were contested: one from Oregon and nineteen from the three Southern states still occupied by Federal troops under command of President Grant, who was soon to be out of office in disgrace. (Florida had four electoral votes, Louisiana eight and South Carolina seven.) After the election results became known, people across the nation engaged in acrimonious confrontations made worse because the disputed Southern states were still occupied and many feared the eruption of another civil war that would prove worse than the first. Nobody knew how things would turn out until long after election day.

The election was violent. There was no registration and fraud was perpetrated by both sides. In Charleston, whites escorted black Democrats to the polls through mobs of club-wielding blacks, who shrieked, "Kill um! Kill um."

On November 8, Charleston had its last race riot—an event precipitated by the actions of the always controversial E.W.M. Mackey. After gleefully reading the election results reported in Republican newspapers to a crowd of illiterate blacks on Broad Street, Mackey strolled up the street to the *News & Courier* bulletin board to gloat some more.

Mackey was described as having the "most horrible and exasperating laugh of any human being in the world—opened his mouth and croaked and barked in his throat, without a sign of mirth on his face or gleam of it through the heavy spectacles that covered his eyes."[51]

A disgusted drunk who heard Mackey's bragging hit him in the face with a hat. During the scuffle that ensued, a pistol shot was discharged accidentally. Blacks standing nearby who had not seen what happened raised the alarm that Mackey had been killed, and an angry mob, joined by renegade policemen, converged at Meeting and Broad Streets. From behind the brick pillars of the old Guard House on Broad Street, they shot every white man they saw. One policeman ambushed an unsuspecting white businessman, Endicott Walker, who was returning to work after dinner.

Once news of the riot spread uptown, army regulars at Marion Square assembled. Members of the local rifle clubs hastened to join them. As the Charleston men fell into position beside them, the Yankee troops cheered and the Southerners responded with the Rebel yell. They marched side by side to disperse the mob. A frightening roar from the scene could be heard many blocks away.

The riot involved over one thousand armed blacks, among whom were the lawless thugs called Hunkidories, five hundred rifle club members and regulars in the United States Army. Although the turbulence lasted for several hours, it is fortunate that only young Walker's life was lost.

Once the South Carolina election results were reported, both sides claimed victory, accusing the other of fraud. Suddenly, the nation sensed that the presidential election hinged on the Palmetto State. Politicians, journalists and illustrators flocked to Columbia.

By South Carolina law, the election was to be determined by the Board of Canvassers, three of whom were up for reelection. Democrats appealed to the state Supreme Court, which ruled, rather surprisingly, that the legislative results published immediately after the election were valid and that the seated legislators would determine the contested sealed votes for governor and lieutenant governor.

The Board of Canvassers defied the ruling and threw out the elections of two Hampton strongholds, Edgefield and Laurens Counties. This gave the Republicans a heavy majority. The canvassers were later arrested on charges of contempt, but were released almost immediately upon the instructions of a sitting Supreme Court justice, who had come down from Washington to observe the proceedings.

Taking no chances while the election results were being disputed, President Grant declared South Carolina to be in a state of rebellion. On November 26, he ordered military and naval forces to support the Republican government. In Columbia that evening, by stealth in the dark of night, a company of infantry was posted inside the statehouse.

By chance, a group of reporters discovered the troops' presence in the statehouse and quickly telegraphed their "scoop" across the nation. Nothing like this had ever occurred before, and numerous newspaper editorials in other parts of the country expressed outrage that federal soldiers would oversee an election in the United States.

On November 27, Governor Chamberlain's deputy personally ordered the soldiers to refuse entry to the Democratic legislators from Edgefield and Laurens Counties.

Hundreds of men had already come to Columbia to witness the opening session of the legislature on November 28. When news that soldiers were occupying the capitol building and that certain Democrats were denied entry reached nearby communities, more of Hampton's supporters hastened into town. By noon, more than five thousand armed and angry men had converged on the capitol grounds, just waiting for the word to attack.

Governor Chamberlain and the army were outnumbered and powerless to prevent bloodshed. Only the restrained intervention of Wade Hampton saved the day. He calmly addressed the crowd and ended his 125-word appeal for order by saying, "I have been elected your governor, and, so help me God, I will take my seat." Mollified, the men dispersed within three minutes. Years later, Hampton reflected to a reporter that "nothing which had yet happened to us was so appalling as that mob, which was friendly to me."[52]

Once order was restored, the rejected House Democrats convened at Carolina Hall, three blocks away from the capitol building, and elected General W.H. Wallace as their speaker.

Meanwhile, at the statehouse, E.W.M. Mackey was elected the Republican Speaker in an assembly of but three whites. Later to be known as the "Mackey House," the Republican legislators began to organize and adjourned until three o'clock the next afternoon, when they would convene to elect their governor.

On Thursday, November 30 (Thanksgiving), the Democratic legislators decided to "storm" the statehouse. Walking down several streets in twos and threes so as not to attract attention, they joined forces at the capitol and walked en masse through the entrance doors. Surprising the House doormen, they gained entrance to the chamber without incident. General Wallace marched straight to the Speaker's desk and took the chair.

The Republicans, who had just begun to assemble, watched in astonishment as the Democrats seated themselves. When Speaker Mackey heard the news, he angrily rushed into the chamber and attempted to have the Democrats evicted. A courteous but tense interchange followed.

Somebody had the presence of mind to offer Mackey a seat, and both he and Wallace sat down on the Speaker's stand. Colonel Haskell, who had suggested "storming the House," sat behind the two men. When Mackey inquired why Haskell was sitting there, he told him that although he did not ordinarily carry a gun, he would kill Mackey if he caused any trouble.

Thus began one of the strangest episodes in legislative history. On each side of the House chamber, two legislative bodies with two duly elected Speakers simultaneously went through the motions of conducting business in noisy cacophony. Each side formally attempted to remove the other to no avail. White upstate men known to be "kinder handy with a gun" somehow obtained entry passes and monitored Speaker Mackey's every move.

Afraid of losing their advantage, both parties remained in the assembly chamber day and night on Thursday, Friday and Saturday. Pistols and rifles were smuggled in. Armed soldiers continued to be posted in the building. Impatient for Hampton to be sworn in, men began to drift back into the city. It was a volatile situation that couldn't sustain itself for long. On the surface, however, all was calm, and on Sunday night the legislators and reporters bedded down at about eleven o'clock.

Nobody knows for sure who warned Wade Hampton late Sunday afternoon of Mackey's plot to forcibly evict the Democrats from the House chamber with the aid of the unruly Hunkidories, who had been hastily summoned from Charleston. When investigated, about one hundred fully armed Hunkidories, duly sworn in as deputy sergeants-at-arms, were found concealed in the committee rooms awaiting their orders.

The Democrats inside the House chamber were outnumbered almost three to one, and it promised to be a massacre. It was speculated that Governor Chamberlain may not have wanted a shootout in the House on his conscience—or in the national news. His authorized biography was strangely silent on this subject.

Knowing trouble was imminent, an emergency call was sent out, and throughout Sunday night the Red Shirts began to arrive. They rode on mules and they rode horseback; they came by regular and special trains. The first influx was from nearby Richland, Lexington and Fairfield. By dawn, the entire capitol building was surrounded, and by noon they were twenty-five hundred strong.

Obeying orders directly from Washington, the occupying army general demanded that the Democrats vacate the capitol. Amid a protest of governmental interference, the Democrats adjourned to Choral Hall shortly after noon. As had been done the previous week, the press of both persuasions had a field day telegraphing their reports across the nation.

Men kept arriving throughout day—four to five thousand taut and angry former soldiers eager to right old wrongs and prepared to fight to the finish. Once again Hampton dispersed the crowd with only a few words. His restraint and command of the situation gained him the respect and sympathy of people across the nation.

The same day, even though it lacked a quorum, the Mackey House elected Chamberlain governor.

On December 6, the state Supreme Court formally declared Hampton the winner of the gubernatorial election. Chamberlain refused to concede and was sworn in on the seventh. Ironically, Mackey's uncle, Judge Thomas Jefferson Mackey, administered the oath of office to Governor Hampton on December 14.

It took five months for Hampton to secure the withdrawal of occupying troops and gain control of the capitol building. By the time the troops had left, South Carolina had been an occupied territory for twelve horrendous years. Some of the occupying troops were black and had been billeted in the mansions of their former foes, causing further hatred.

The Mackey House supported would-be governor Chamberlain until he finally vacated on April 10, 1877. From then until he died in 1884, Mackey tried unsuccessfully to resuscitate the Republican Party in South Carolina.

Demonstration of the citizens upon the return of Wade Hampton, April 6, 1877. *Courtesy Library of Congress.*

As things turned out, in all three contested Southern states, the Republican election boards threw out enough Democratic votes to give the election to Hayes and the Republican gubernatorial candidates. Louisiana and South Carolina Democrats declared their gubernatorial candidates elected, established rival state administrations and certified Tilden as the winner in their states. The Florida Supreme Court ruled in favor of the Democratic gubernatorial candidate, but let Hayes's margin of victory stand. The new Florida governor promptly appointed a Democratic election board that announced Tilden had carried the state.

Numbers 24 and 26 New Street are silent reminders of Reconstruction and the enmity it created among the defeated.

OTHER HAPPENINGS

After Mackey's death, 24 New Street was turned into a boardinghouse run by Grandma Walters. She had been a

Hazlehurst before her marriage and had also run a boardinghouse on Sullivan's Island in the late nineteenth century. Charles F. Middleton Jr. (Fanfan) boarded temporarily at 24 New Street after a business debacle in Savannah.

Charles F. Middleton III purchased 24 New Street in December 1919. His wife, Margaret S. Middleton, purchased a portrait by Jeremiah Theus, which still hangs in the front parlor. The art dealer who sold it to her had been sworn to secrecy and never revealed the provenance of the painting in spite of many requests. She always attributed the subject to be someone in the Barnwell family because of his likeness to some of the Barnwells of her generation.

Number 24 New Street boasts the grand piano that the Polish statesman and pianist Ignacy Jan Paderewski played when he visited Charleston. His hands were so powerful that he broke the sounding board, and the owner, Mayor Rhett, put the piano up for sale at Siegling's Music House, where the senior Middleton bought it for his granddaughter, Dorothy.

During the 1940 primary election, Marwee Middleton and her husband, L. Mendel Rivers, lived on the ground floor of 24 New Street, while Rivers contested the candidate of the Charleston Democratic Party machine for the congressional seat. Charleston police, the mayor, and his minions may have behaved shamefully, but their chicanery was nothing compared to the hair-raising days of 1876. Like Hampton, Rivers won hugely outside of Charleston County, where votes were once again blatantly stolen.

Number 24 New Street has also experienced great sadness. Simons Hasell, a nephew of Mrs. Middleton, was accidentally killed one Sunday afternoon. The chauffer employed to help Fanfan with his sciatica was playing in the backyard with the Middleton cousins. As the boys ran through a hail of bullets he shot from a .22 rifle, young Simons was fatally hit.

Charles Francis Middleton III was drowned off the coast of Virginia during marine maneuvers in the Second World War, leaving behind a pregnant wife and one son. The family never fully recovered from his death.

Charlie Middleton in the 1930s. *Courtesy College of Charleston Library (Rivers Family Collection).*

Number 26 New Street remained in the Hayne family until it was bought by Alfred and Julianna Pinckney in January 1974. Pinckney is a direct descendant of Roger Pinckney, who had come to the province as the Crown provost marshal.

TOOTIN' THE BOUL

48 Murray Boulevard

There is a small, circumspect generation of people who grew up between the Great Depression and the Baby Boomers. Their ideas of teenage rebellion were James Dean, smoking cigarettes and "dirty dancing" to rock 'n roll. They were the last vestiges of Victorianism and its sexual morality.

In Charleston one of the rites of passage was being old enough to drive the family car, something permitted at fourteen in those days. Carefree adolescents would happily drive back and forth on Murray Boulevard, also known as the Low Battery, "tootin' the Boul." This heady independence sometimes included dropping off younger siblings at Mrs. Whaley's dancing school at the South Carolina Hall on Meeting Street, where little girls wore white gloves and boys donned coats and ties while they learned the intricacies of ballroom dancing.

Mere children, these innocents were not sophisticated enough to appreciate the enormous effort that had been required to fill in the mud flats and marshes that created the splendid drive beside the Ashley River as it flows into Charleston Harbor. Nor did the youngsters care about what might have happened behind the handsome façades of the newly built homes facing the water.

It was years before Charlestonians learned about wartime foreign intrigue that had once been part of the Charleston streetscape. And as chance would have it, this delicious tale was

An aerial view of Murray Boulevard, circa 1927. *Courtesy Carlton Simons.*

connected to a Middleton residence on Murray Boulevard. *The Buildings of Charleston* describes number 48 Murray as a neoclassical revival mansion "constructed by a leading cotton exporting family about 1929" and goes on to say that "in 1942, while stationed in Charleston, Lt. John F. Kennedy lived in the garage apartment at the rear of the lot."[53] This account needs some modification.

Young Abbott Middleton remembered well when the family moved into their new home because it was his ninth birthday, November 1, 1928. Construction on the home had suddenly halted after a disastrous cotton purchase had almost bankrupted Middleton & Company, and money had suddenly run out. As a result of the belt tightening, no wash basin was installed in the downstairs powder room. When friends would "wash their hands," the family would jokingly chat about what their guests were thinking while using a powder room with only toilet facilities.

Dr. Barnwell (Barney) Rhett lived next door, and he had built a dock in front of his house. After a storm took it away, he replaced it with a much sturdier version that lasted until the city finally had it removed in the 1950s. The Rhett, Farrow, Middleton and Huger children swam from the dock and enjoyed sailing from

Sailing in the 1930s. *Courtesy College of Charleston Library (Rivers Family Collection).*

the boats moored nearby. About fifty feet from the sea wall were the bateaux, and about one hundred yards farther out were two sailboats and three launches, each about thirty to thirty-five feet. The boys sometimes sailed to the still-undeveloped Kiawah Island for camping adventures on the beach. They fished, crabbed and shrimped in the bountiful waters and feasted on the hominy grits they took along as their only provision. It was a fun and carefree existence. "Back then everybody was dead broke, but they just didn't know it," Abbott Middleton reminisced years later.

As was done in many homes during World War II, the Middletons had several naval officers live in their home. The young men were delighted to lodge in nice private homes instead of the crowded bachelor officers' quarters at the navy yard. Ordinarily, the Middleton "guests" used the vacant third-floor bedroom that belonged to young Abbott, who was away in the service. The Middleton girls had married and moved away by then, and Mrs. Middleton's mother was staying in one of the vacant second-floor bedrooms.

As a special favor to one of their lodgers, the Middletons gave the unoccupied water-view room to a young ensign. He was the handsome son of a prestigious Massachusetts political family. As coincidence would have it, Jack Kennedy had met the Middletons' youngest daughter, Lois, through a boarding school friend, Nedenia "Deenie" Hutton (stage name Dina Merrill). Young Lois forewarned her mother about Kennedy's reputation with the ladies. When he rang the doorbell, he greeted Mrs. Middleton with "Where's Loddie?" As only Lois's close friends used her nickname, the surprised Mrs. Middleton tersely replied, "She is a married woman, and her name is Lois."

At first the Middleton's were delighted to have Jack Kennedy staying with them. That is, until Joe Kennedy sent his son a set of four brand-new, white-walled tires for his sports car. Young Kennedy arranged to be present when they arrived and had them stored in the Middleton basement. Not only was it presumptuous, but it was also distasteful for, due to wartime rubber shortages,

Mrs. Middleton's car had been jacked up in the garage after the tires became worn and could not be replaced. This had happened to cars all over town.

When young Abbott returned on leave from the U.S. Air Force, he was obliged to stay in one of his married sister's rooms because by then Kennedy was using his room on the third floor. Abbott found Kennedy to be an extremely personable young man who fit in well with the convivial neighborhood partying atmosphere.

Kennedy left suddenly under rather strained circumstances. The only upstairs phone was located in the hall. Jack Kennedy was quite popular and received a call just as he finished showering. Henny Whaley, Mrs. Middleton's mother, who was upstairs, answered the phone. She knocked on his door to inform him of the call, and he dashed out, clad only in a towel wrapped around his waist. Mrs. Whaley was one of Charleston's *grande dames*, someone who was used to being awarded every social courtesy and respect. Having a young man appear without his clothes on just wasn't proper, and she gave him a "piece of her mind" in what must have been a most imperious fashion. Not too long after that, Jack Kennedy relocated to a house on Sullivan's Island, taking Mrs. Middleton's newly trained maid with him.

The Middletons would have had even less use for Ensign Jack if they had known a little more about his comings and goings. What the circumspect household did not think to question was why an attractive naval intelligence officer had been transferred from the gay social life of the nation's capitol to a dull desk job in Charleston, South Carolina. If they had, they would have been shocked to learn that Kennedy was deeply involved with a beautiful, twenty-eight-year-old Danish news journalist, Inga Arvad. She had known connections with high-ranking Nazis and was under scrutiny as a suspected spy. The navy looked at her as similar to Mata Hari.

Before coming to Charleston, Ensign Kennedy had been working for the Office of Naval Intelligence when his sister Kathleen (Kick) Kennedy introduced him to her roommate. She

Boys boating in the country. *Courtesy Middleton family.*

was beautiful, worldly and a challenge to the spoiled, handsome scion of a powerful political family. Jack and Inga became inseparable. This was no casual fling! Joe Kennedy became afraid that Jack might actually marry the divorced, non-Catholic Inga. FBI Director J. Edgar Hoover hated Joe Kennedy and wanted to curtail his ambitions to set up a political dynasty. When young Kennedy took up with Arvad, Hoover had the couple tailed, photographed and even recorded their pillow talk. Jack affectionately called Arvad "Inga-Binga," and she nicknamed him "Honeysuckle." When the assistant director of the Office of Naval Intelligence found out about the FBI surveillance, he had Kennedy assigned to Charleston.

The lovers' relationship continued in Charleston with a few weekend trysts at the Fort Sumter Hotel, located only a few blocks from the Middleton household. Both Kennedy and Arvad knew they were being recorded, and FBI transcripts sometimes make reference to "whoever is listening." Historians suggest that, throughout his presidency, Kennedy tried unsuccessfully to obtain the FBI recordings. Although the bulk of the surveillance documentation was declassified in the 1990s, some has never been released.

Supposedly, Hoover called the secretary of the navy and said something to the effect of: "We have a problem. A young, well-connected naval officer is having an affair with a German spy and we have the tapes to prove it. I think you should kick him out of the navy."

The secretary of the navy immediately called Joe Kennedy and said, "Joe, Hoover has tapes of Jack having an affair with a German spy and wants me to kick him out of the navy"

Joe replied, "For God's sake, don't do that—just get him as far from that damn woman as quickly as possible."

So, Ensign Jack Kennedy was hastily transferred to the West Coast. After six months' training, he was promoted to lieutenant early in 1943 and shipped out to the Pacific theatre. The rest is history.

An interesting footnote to the story is that "Loddie" (Lois Middleton Stoney) later lived at 29 East Battery, the imposing, three-story, Greek revival mansion that was remodeled in the Beaux Arts and Renaissance revival style in 1894. During World War II, the U.S. Office of Naval Intelligence used the house and enclosed the side piazzas. Coincidentally, Jack Kennedy worked there during his tenure in Charleston.[54]

Every winter after the war, while en route to Florida, Deenie Hutton's mother used to stop by Charleston to visit the Middletons when they still lived at 48 Murray Boulevard. Her private yacht, the *Sea Cloud*, would anchor in the Ashley River close to Dr. Rhett's dock. It must have been quite a sight to see a ship over two hundred feet long with high masts dwarfing the boulevard mansions.

The Middletons later sold their home to an orthodontist, Dr. Joseph Lawson Johnson, who had moved from Spartanburg. Joe and Vivian Johnson became friends of the Middletons. Their son Joe married Beverly Stoney, Abbott Middleton's granddaughter.

SCANDAL ON
MEETING STREET

61 Meeting Street

Without question, Meeting Street is one of Charleston's most prestigious and historic streets. Getting its name from the meetinghouse built in 1685,[55] it has been the scene of commercial, religious and social activities since that time. In 1704, when the early colonists were forced to build a protective wall against pirates and Spanish raiding parties, the drawbridge and moat were located at the corner of Broad and Meeting Streets.[56]

Before the Revolution, a statue of William Pitt was erected at the crossing of Meeting and Broad amid the wild enthusiasm of a local populace who appreciated their Parliamentary defender in the Stamp Act crisis as passionately as they opposed taxation without representation.[57] Ninety years later, South Carolina seceded from the Union on Meeting Street. This busy street has hosted parades and seen soldiers march down it to quell Charleston's race riots.

Known as the "Corner of Four Laws," the intersection at Broad and Meeting Streets is still one of the premier locations in the city. St. Michael's Church dominates the other handsome public buildings, promoting the fanciful suggestion that as the sun runs its course in the sky each day, the shadow of the church's spire falls on each of its neighbors—the federal post office, the county courthouse and the city hall—symbolic of God's rule over all the laws of man.

Built in 1752–61, St. Michael's Church is an architectural treasure. This landmark was the second monumental colonial church patterned after St. Martin-in-the-Fields, London. *Courtesy St. Michael's Church.*

In 1938, a tornado blew a hole in the roof of St. Michael's. An irreverent Charlestonian declared it an "Act of God" because, he said, "God had been trying to get into St. Michael's for two hundred years."

The Middleton family attended St. Michael's Church because, as the family patriarch put it, "the Episcopal Church did not interfere with either your religion or your politics."

Back in the 1930s, the old families rented their pews. If an innocent visitor found a seat for himself when the ushers were busy on a crowded Sunday, usually Christmas or Easter, the pew tenants would not ask the offender to leave. Instead, they would make the newcomer feel isolated, unwelcome and most uncomfortable, trusting that he received the message to never repeat the offense. There were parishioners who attended only at Easter and yet considered themselves absolutely entitled to the exclusive use of their pews after having rented, and ignored, them for a whole year. They were called the "Easter Lilies."

There is also the story about a youngster who wanted to attend St. Michael's Sunday school. The mother protested, "You go to a nice Sunday school." Whereupon the child replied, "But Mother, you don't understand. At our Sunday school, all we hear about is God, and Jesus and the Bible. But at St. Michael's, it's different. They *never* talk about those things."[58]

Slightly south of St. Michael's is the imposing South Carolina Hall, recognized as one of the finest examples of Federal architecture in the nation. And proceeding on to White Point Gardens is Charleston's most exclusive residential area. The essential information about many imposing mansions is discretely noted on unobtrusive plaques attached to their façades.

Charlestonians are proud of their heritage and all it represents. They love the good life, their eccentric "characters" and a risqué joke. For the most part, they are very circumspect. And like most people, they enjoy a little gossip. The scandalous events connected with number 61 Meeting Street, however, are something Charlestonians would prefer to forget.

Before World War II, Charleston was a closed society, and living South of Broad was mandatory for social acceptability. Lower Meeting Street was inhabited by very proper ladies and gentlemen who would never have tolerated interfering "damnyankees."

Number 61 Meeting Street, located diagonally south of the South Carolina Hall, is the converted stable of the Branford-Horry House. For many years, this attractive, unassuming stucco home was the residence of Federal Judge Julius Waties Waring.

Judge Waring had impeccable social and professional credentials. He was a member of one of Charleston's finest families. Born in 1880, he was the son of Edward Perry Waring, a veteran of the War Between the States, having marched southward as a Citadel cadet to defend Charleston from Sherman's army.

A quiet man who paid attention to detail, Waring served as attorney for the City of Charleston and handled himself well. He had a reputation as a local kingmaker, as he was chairman of the Charleston County Democratic Party. When he was nominated to the federal bench, his nomination was supported by all who knew him. In spite of his age, Waring was easily confirmed by the U.S. Senate and became the local federal judge. He was sixty-one, and his wife was justly proud of his appointment.

Waring had married Annie Gammell in 1913, and two years later the couple moved into the house she owned at 61 Meeting Street. She was considered a good wife and a good mother.

Prior to their marriage, Annie Gammell had studied drama in New York, where she became infatuated with the celebrated actress Sarah Bernhardt. At the actress's invitation, she spent four winters in Paris enjoying the theatre and being included in Bernhardt's household activities.

The Waties Warings appeared to be the ideal couple. As part of Charleston's elite, they had a nice circle of friends. They entertained often at their Meeting Street home. An invitation to their New Year's Eve party was a social must. Waring's daughter made her début at the St. Cecilia Society in 1937.

Then the Hoffmans came to town. Henry Hoffman was from Rhode Island, and he was extremely wealthy. He was twenty years older than his wife Elizabeth. It was common knowledge that she had married Hoffman the day after her Reno divorce decree from her first husband, Wilson Mills, a prominent lawyer from Detroit.

The Hoffmans always wintered a couple of months in Charleston. They stayed at only the best places, first at the Villa Margherita and subsequently at other downtown homes.[59] They met and mingled with the locals. They played bridge with their Charleston friends. Judge Waring and his wife Annie were part of that crowd.

Elizabeth Hoffman was not like the conservative Charleston ladies. She was rich and generally regarded as "a handsome, charming woman with considerable sex appeal."[60] She was also intelligent and strong-willed. She considered herself "party material," an attribute she thought local Charlestonians admired.

The judge already had a reputation for being a rake with a wandering eye. He had the nickname "King of the Tenderloin District," which meant that he frequented houses of ill repute.[61] In the course of time, he and Elizabeth were attracted to one another, fell in love and had a torrid affair. Charleston insiders were not surprised. It was said that when Elizabeth would enter his courtroom, all work stopped, as the judge couldn't take his eyes off of her.

One day, Judge Waring came home and announced to his wife that he wanted a divorce. As South Carolina was the only state in the nation where divorces were illegal, she was to go to Florida, establish residence and not come back until she got one. She meekly said, "Yes, Waties," and did his bidding, quickly getting on a train heading south. According to Bradish J. Waring, his grandfather, Simons Vanderhorst Waring, took the next train to Florida and succeeded in bringing Annie back to Charleston temporarily. Eventually, she returned to the Sunshine State, staying with her husband's sister-in-law in Jacksonville while establishing residency. In Charleston, divorce was considered such a disgrace that during her ordeal, Annie Waring became ill and lost twenty-five pounds.

Judge Waring and the twice-divorced Elizabeth were married a week after his divorce from Annie Gammell. For unknown reasons, Annie moved out of her home and the judge retained his residence at 61 Meeting Street. Used to dispensing power, the judge believed he could simply tell Annie to go, and all would be well. She did, but there were repercussions.

Charleston ladies hated Elizabeth Waring. She was called the "witch of Meeting Street," although some used a slightly different word. She is still remembered for having a wild mane of black hair, cheap-looking, very tight skirts and blouses and far too much makeup. Her face was heavily rouged, and her lipstick was a bright red painted beyond the borders of her natural lips. Worse yet, she wore platform high heels, usually with no backs, and they flapped against her feet as she walked down the street. Red painted nails peeked through the open toes of her shoes.

Divorce in that day was rare. It was the social kiss of death if one were a member of the St. Cecilia Society, which, up until the early twenty-first century, would not allow a previously divorced member to bring any new wife to the annual ball. This was old Charleston's way of sending a message. Some cowered and took the medicine and others, perhaps like Judge Waring, took the snub as a challenge to create a new life under the noses of old friends. Some of Waring's family believe he was operating in part under the "cornered-animal syndrome," through which the beast that is given no other options to save its life lashes out viciously at the throat of its attacker. Other family members emphasize that Charleston society turned on the judge solely for the manner in which he treated his former wife.

Regardless of why and how it happened, Waring gradually distanced himself from his family and alienated his friends. The newly wed Warings became social pariahs. One story was that Waring invited all his downtown Charleston friends to a party and not one appeared. According to some Waring family members, Judge Waring turned on old friends who tried to be cordial, refusing to grant them entrance to his home or office, though it is uncertain when participants drew lines in the social sand.

Informed speculation aside, nobody knows exactly what happened to Waring, but after he married Elizabeth Hoffman, he became a liberal—at least considered so in his day—setting a course beyond the map of the Southern culture in which he grew up.

Judge Waring issued highly controversial rulings about race in his hometown that made his white friends and family angry. He issued rulings declaring the whites-only Democratic primary to be unconstitutional and requiring that blacks be allowed to vote in the primary. He encouraged the U.S. Attorney's Office to prosecute white officials accused of injuring black men. Another highlight of Judge Waring's judicial career was writing a dissenting opinion as part of a three-federal-judge panel reviewing *Briggs v. Elliott, et al* (Clarendon County Board of Education) in which Thurgood Marshall, representing the NAACP, argued on behalf of the plaintiff. Judge Waring's opinion, declaring the segregated Clarendon County public schools unconstitutional, was eventually affirmed, as Briggs was part of the U.S. Supreme Court's *Brown v. Board of Education* decision.

Judge Waring's impact in local legal circles persists to this day. Retired Circuit Judge Richard Fields often tells about one of his first appearances before Judge Waring, when he represented an alleged black bootlegger and Ben Scott Whaley was an assistant U.S. district attorney. Assuming that Judge Waring knew who Richard Fields was, Whaley did not introduce him, but rather recited the plea agreement that had been worked out with the defendant. After a long and awkward silence, Judge Waring asked what the other fellow (Richard Fields) had done. Once the embarrassing mistake was explained, Judge Fields said that he knew his client was not going to jail.

Not to be outdone, Elizabeth Waring made a speech at the Charleston YWCA in which she proclaimed that white Southerners were (and these are her words) "degenerate." She said that they were prejudiced and backward and must learn to accept the Negro into their schools, their hearts and their lives, as equals. Due to the news coverage, she quickly became a celebrity elsewhere and repeated her views in an interview on *Meet the Press*. There was enormous backlash. It was said that the Warings feared for their lives. They asked for protection from the FBI. There were some claims that the Klan threw brickbats at the house, but it turned out that it was only mischievous neighborhood boys, at least one of whom grew up to become a prominent criminal defense attorney.

The judge's nephew, Thomas R. Waring Jr., was editor of Charleston's morning newspaper, the *News & Courier*, but the family connection did not give the judge any favoritism in print; rather, it may have had the opposite effect. In Charles Rowe's *Pages of History: 200 Years of The Post and Courier*, he claimed that "Waring's (T.R.'s) colleagues contend that the liberal record of his uncle…made the editor more conservative on issues related to desegregation." The editorials irritated the judge to the point where he would not speak to his nephew.

Upon his uncle's elevation to a judgeship, another nephew, Charles W. Waring, resigned as a federal attorney in Washington, D.C., and returned to his native Charleston to take Waties Waring's place in the law firm of Waring and Brockinton. Soft-spoken Charles Waring, known as "Boo" to his friends, did not champion or vilify his uncle in public.

Some politicians spoke up. One of the most aggressive was the local United States congressman. He turned up the heat on Waring as much as he could. He wrote to the chief justice of the United States, Fred Vinson, and asked him to initiate an investigation against Judge Waring, with a view toward discipline. Vinson declined, stating that there needed to be a formal complaint, and some grounds, to commence an investigation. The congressman tried to have Waring impeached and ran into the same problem: Waring hadn't committed any crime or any ethical breach. The congressman made speeches on the floor of the House, criticizing both of the Warings, and got his name in the local papers. But

Congressman Mendel Rivers turned up the heat on Waring as much as he could. *Courtesy College of Charleston Library (Rivers Collection).*

like the ostracism of the downtowners, the negative attacks had no effect.[62]

Eventually, the Warings' social circle was limited to black folks, including members of the NAACP. They entertained their new friends on a grand scale. Almost every Sunday, across the street from St. Michael's Church, departing parishioners could see a line of "colored people" waiting to get into Judge Waring's home. Dressed up in their Sunday best, the crowd was loud and could not be ignored. It was quite a spectacle, for the line stretched almost to Broad Street.

Throughout it all, the first Mrs. Waring lived on $250 a month at 80½ Tradd Street, in the rented "kitchen house" of a prominent doctor who lived around the corner from her former home. Reduced in financial means and humiliated by divorce, she was ignored by many of those she had once considered friends. She must have found her new circumstances extremely difficult, for she could see her ex-husband and the flashy younger wife prance around the corner to the ground floor of the dependency of 79 Tradd Street, where they parked their car. (The house has since been demolished to make room for the parishioner parking of First Scots Presbyterian Church.)

After her divorce, Annie Waring lived like a recluse and rarely went anywhere. She was often bedridden. She took great joy, however, in entertaining the daughter of the doctor who owned the big house with her tales of faraway places and her days with the famous actress. Her only companion was a dog named Wee Willie Winkey.

Locals still laugh about how Annie Waring got her revenge. She could be seen walking Wee Willie Winkey on Meeting Street, where the obliging dog sniffed the front door of his former home and left his wet calling card in disdain.

One day, the gentle Annie Waring quietly left. A painful reminder of an unpleasant time in Charleston history, her departure seemed to have been mourned only by the little girl whom she had charmed with her stories about the celebrated actress Sarah Bernhardt and the interesting life she had once lived. She died in 1954 and was buried in Magnolia Cemetery at her parents' gravesite. All but one of her pallbearers were members of the Waring family.[63]

As for the judge and Elizabeth, they retained their residence on Meeting Street. The downtown ladies referred to Elizabeth as a "floozie," something that sounded almost exotic to the youngsters who were admonished to be polite when spoken to, but never to address her. The Warings entertained their black friends until the judge retired. Then they moved to New York City and became fixtures at cocktail parties given by civil rights activists, including Harry Belafonte.

Judge Waring returned to Charleston only once. He stayed with Ruby Cornwell, now deceased, a black civil rights activist married to a dentist who lived on Congress Street. (Sources do not say if Elizabeth accompanied her husband.) Attorney Thomas Waring, son of the late editor, interviewed Mrs. Cornwell and learned that the judge had come back to be honored at an NAACP dinner. Because of concerns for his safety, Waring had stayed with Ruby and her husband instead of at a hotel.

After his death in 1968, like any proper Charlestonian, Judge Waring was buried in Magnolia Cemetery. Charles Kuralt covered the funeral for *CBS News* and chased down Waring family members for comments. As was to be expected, reporters are not welcome at a Charleston funeral, especially in 1968, and the family refused to go on camera or remark about the passing of their controversial kinsman. Elizabeth Avery Waring died later the same year and is buried beside Judge Waring in Magnolia Cemetery.

In spite of their political differences, after Waring's death his family exhibited the age-old respect for the deceased, especially for one of their own. Nearly forty years later, and long after Simons Vanderhorst Waring would cross Broad Street to avoid having to speak to Judge Waring, Simons Waring's grandson, Bradish J. Waring, and Thomas Waring, son of the editor who vilified his uncle's judicial decisions, represented the family at the South Carolina Bar's "Memory Hold the Door" ceremony when Judge Waring was inducted in 2004.

CLOSING THE DOOR
ON AN ERA
13 East Battery

O nce the safety of American shipping was ensured after the War of 1812, American commerce began to recover from the decline it suffered during the Revolution and afterward. This was especially true in Charleston, where the exportation of naval stores, rice and Sea Island cotton produced unimaginable wealth, making Charleston one of the richest cities in the nation.

With their newfound affluence, the city fathers devised a grand scheme for a gathering place for Charleston's elite—an elegant, L-shaped park that extended from Atlantic to Church Streets on the east and faced South Battery on the south. The land was part of the Oyster Point shoreline, which extended beyond the original walled city at the southern end of the peninsula. The park was envisioned to be a "public pleasure ground" called White Point Gardens.

Before the development plans were implemented, the financial panic of 1837 caused the city to modify its original design. The city fathers decided to raise the money for a somewhat smaller park by selling off the land on the eastern side of the proposed project. The remaining parkland was a spacious rectangle that eventually extended all the way to King Street.

The city sold the eastern land to some of Charleston's most successful businessmen with the expectation that they would build a beautiful row of ornamental homes opposite the high retaining wall along what is now called East Battery or the High Battery. It is here that some of Charleston's most glorious mansions were built before the war.

The first residence was a handsome, brick, Greek revival house built by William Roper. It was sited on the lot at a slight angle so that, with nothing to obstruct the view, the five massive Ionic columns on the piazza could be seen from miles away by the sailors coming into the harbor.

Shortly thereafter, William Ravenel, the owner of one of Charleston's major steamship lines, built a handsome Greek revival mansion to the north of Roper's residence. The Ravenel home was equally impressive, with a beautiful, two-story portico supported by fluted, Tower of the Winds Corinthian columns that faced the sea.[64] The intricate stucco work in the drawing room was done by an Irishman, and the woodwork—including the huge, two-panel, ten-foot doors—was executed by Ravenel's slave carpenters.

The Ravenel family was descended from Huguenots who came to the Carolinas in the 1680s. They were respected members of the French Protestant congregation and took great care to preserve their heritage by speaking and reading French at home. The Ravenel family was well established by the time of the American Revolution.

The family has preserved some charming anecdotes of Revolutionary times. A favorite was about the British attempt to steal an exceptionally fine horse belonging to Daniel Ravenel of Wantoot plantation in St. John's Parish, about six miles from Pinopolis. A slave overseer heard of the British intention and put the horse in one room of his two-room house. He removed the floorboards in the room to conceal any noise that might be made by the horse's hooves. When the British demanded to know the whereabouts of the horse, he was afraid that the horse would neigh; however, he was able to maintain his composure when he told the British that he knew "Nuttin' 'bout de hos'." In recounting the tale to the family later, he "tanked de Lord w'en dem British gone. He nearly kill heself with de laf at foolin' dem British."[65]

Number 13 East Battery before the earthquake. *Courtesy Edith Corry.*

Shortly after the Revolution, General William Moultrie took a shortcut when he rode home one night. At Simons Hill near Wantoot, Moultrie thought he saw "the Devil" ride beside him. Suddenly, something with fiery eyes seemed to go before, beside and behind his terrified horse. Not being able to determine exactly

129

what the apparition was, Moultrie had become extremely agitated by the time he reached Wantoot. He told the Ravenels about the incident, and the next day they investigated the area where the apparition had appeared. They surmised that "the Devil" must have been a phosphorescent light that appeared in the night over the marshy grounds and swamps in the region. Upon being questioned about it later, Moultrie bemoaned the fact that this "story will never die."[66]

By the time of the heyday of Charleston's prosperity between the 1840s and "The War," the sons of Daniel Ravenel II were all prominent members of the community. Daniel Ravenel was chairman of the committee sent to bring the remains of John C. Calhoun to Charleston and for years was president of the Planters and Mechanics Bank. Brother Henry was president of the Union Bank, and as a captain in the Washington Light Infantry, he went to Florida in the Seminole War. Brother Edmund was an eminent doctor, chemist and amateur conchologist of international standing, as well as being one of the founders of the Medical College of South Carolina. Not only was brother John president of the South Carolina Railroad, but he and brother William also had a large shipping business called Ravenel & Company. It was considered to be among the exporting firms that were instrumental in contributing to the prewar prosperity of the South.[67]

William Ravenel was born in 1806 and married Eliza Butler Pringle in 1836. They had eleven children. Ravenel was educated in Charleston and entered the counting room of Ravenel and Stevens in 1823, where he learned how to receive and sell the planters' staples. Eventually the firm entered into the lucrative foreign trade.

Ravenel was so successful in commerce that he built a handsome mansion overlooking the harbor and moved his family to number 7 (now number 13) East Battery in 1845. Family tradition states that he loved to watch his ships sail over the bar into the protected waters of Charleston Harbor. Ravenel owned a country place west of the Ashley known as Farmfield, and after Roper's death, he purchased the house next door.

Like other members of the upper class, life for the Ravenels was a pleasant combination of civic leadership, social intercourse and making money—lots of money. Like their peers, they were totally unprepared for what lay ahead when war started and their idyllic lifestyle abruptly stopped.

The Ravenels were forced to move out of their beautiful home after the August 21, 1863 Union bombardment, which began suddenly in the middle of the night. Unlike previous bombardments, this time the buildings on East Battery were hit hard by the unexpected barrage. Somehow Ravenel obtained an ambulance for his dying Confederate cadet son, who had contracted a fever while on guard duty. The family journeyed uptown to the home of George Trenholm, whose luxurious residence on Rutledge Avenue had once belonged to Ravenel's father-in-law, James Reid Pringle. (It is now the showplace of Ashley Hall School.)[68]

By the winter of 1865, the Ravenel family had relocated to Farmfield. Wartime privations had begun to set in and everyone had learned to "make do" with what was available. Things went from bad to worse before the family left Farmfield and joined in the evacuation of Charleston and the dreary days of death and destruction that followed.

In June 1865, Charleston was occupied by three regiments of black troops and one regiment of white troops. The Ravenel house on East Battery was occupied by several Union officers, who had repaired some of the wartime damage so that they could live in comfort in their appropriated quarters.[69]

After "the Confederate War," life was hard and everyone was poor. People lost their properties not only through wartime destruction, but also through taxation and confiscation. Politically bound hand and foot, the defeated people tried to make it a practice to shop only in stores belonging to owners who had supported the Confederacy. Practically all commerce had been destroyed.

When he was in his sixties, William Ravenel reentered business. Under his administration, the struggling Stono Phosphate

Company became extremely prosperous. He was the first president of the Cotton Exchange after the war and was a director of the Planters and Mechanics Bank, where his brother served as president. The Ravenels survived better than most, for they prospered and were surrounded by educated people who enjoyed the gentle arts of conversation, dancing and music. Ravenel was president of the St. Cecilia Society for twenty-five years, as well as being treasurer of the Jockey Club. On a civic note, he was a member of the city council and was active in civic and benevolent activities in the community up until the time of his death in 1888.[70]

Having already survived pirates, British occupation, the Confederate War and the horrors of Reconstruction, Charleston suffered another unimaginable disaster. At 9:51 p.m. on Tuesday, August 31, 1886, the first shock of the Charleston earthquake occurred, accompanied by a deep and frightening subterranean roar. Although estimates of the duration of the tremors vary, they were of a magnitude capable of causing great destruction throughout the city. Most of the mansions on the made land on East Battery had cracked walls and fallen parapets. The spectacular Tower of the Winds Corinthian columns on the William Ravenel House crashed with such force that the capital of one column was discovered under an uprooted tree after a 1950s hurricane.[71]

Once the portico columns at number 13 were destroyed, the overhead roof had nothing to support its weight. Lacking the means to restore the portico to its former glory, the Ravenels removed the roof. A balustrade was later constructed on top of the base of the portico, but it deteriorated and has since been removed. The obvious absence of the portico caused a carriage tour guide to invent his own creative version of how the columns were destroyed. He was overheard telling his gullible guests that during a fierce storm, a ship came over the sea wall and knocked down the columns.

Ravenels continued to live at number 13 through the excitement of entertaining the young men bound for the Spanish American War, the First World War and the women's suffrage movement. The proud Ravenel sisters considered it their responsibility to vote.

Number 13 East Battery after the earthquake. *Courtesy Edith Corry.*

At the ages of seventy-one, seventy-nine, eighty-one and eighty-two, they studied the qualifications of the candidates, registered at the Fireproof Building and cast their first votes on Church Street, having been properly escorted there by their brother, Pringle.

Like many other Charleston mansions, number 13 East Battery ran into "hard times" during the Depression. It remained in the Ravenel family until it was sold to Victor Morawetz, who preserved it from further decay until it was purchased by the Frederick Rutledge Bakers. (Lois Hazlehurst Middleton Baker's husband was employed in her father's cotton brokerage business.)

Mrs. Baker had already renovated two historic homes on King Street. The first was number 54 King, the James Brown House. The Bakers later purchased and renovated 21 King Street, where they enjoyed a luxurious apartment on the second and third floors. After the Bakers moved across the street, 54 King Street was rented out until the property was sold to Susan Rutledge Moore in 1937.

By the time the Bakers purchased 13 East Battery, the house needed just about everything done to it. Light could be seen

Lois Hazlehurst Middleton Baker. *Courtesy College of Charleston Library (Rivers Family Collection).*

through cracks in the floorboards, and plaster was crumbling. After they renovated the house, the hospitable Bakers frequently entertained guests with afternoon tea and cocktails on the balustraded "piazza," where everyone enjoyed the unobstructed harbor view and gentle sea breezes. If asked, Hazel Baker would probably have liked to be remembered for her good taste and wonderful sense of humor; she is still remembered for lining her dresser drawers with satin.

The Bakers' son sold 13 East Battery to Edith and William Corry in 1965. Continuing on in the tradition of the former owners, this elegant mansion is furnished with period furniture and has the gracious ambiance of a mini Winterthur.[72] The second-floor drawing room contains a tasteful collection of decorative arts, hand-crafted American furniture and a high-style Charleston chest-on-chest.

The current owner of 13 East Battery provided an interesting anecdote that was related to her by Mrs. Arthur Ravenel (neé Mary Allen Boykin). It seems that there is a history of the supernatural in the Ravenel family. Not only does Farmfield have a well-publicized ghost, but there have also been other paranormal traditions. William Ravenel's mother-in-law was Elizabeth Mary McPherson, who survived the sinking of the *Rose in Bloom*. While on the voyage, she dreamt three times that the ship would be wrecked in a fierce storm. The third time she had the dream was the night the storm occurred, and she got up and changed from her heavy traveling gown into a lightweight silk dress that she thought would float. During the storm, both she and her father were cast into the sea, where he tragically died. She survived the ordeal just as her dreams had foretold and lived to tell the tale. A handsome wall monument at the Gibbes Art Gallery commemorates the loss of General John McPherson and the sinking of the *Rose in Bloom*.

Here is Mrs. Ravenel's story about number 13 East Battery. After the house was sold, the Ravenels gathered to pack up their belongings. One afternoon, while they were upstairs in the drawing room, they heard the front door open and shut. Then they heard the sound of "deliberate steps" walking down the long foyer below them. Thinking that it was a family member, they ran to the head of the stairs and called down to inquire who was there. All was silent. Then they heard the same "deliberate footsteps" return down the foyer, and the door shut once again.

The family rushed downstairs to investigate. To their amazement, no one was there! Afterward, they decided that the mysterious footsteps must have belonged to an ancestor, someone who had come in to commemorate an end to the long Ravenel residency by "closing the door on an era."

Nosey intruder or Ravenel ghost? You decide.

NOTES

Introduction

1. Attributed to William Watts Ball, editor of the *Charleston News & Courier*.

Street Music

2. Rivers et al., *Mendel and Me*, 45.
3. Rivers, *Fanfan*, 22–23.

The Crown Jewel of Lower Church Street

4. Poston, *Buildings of Charleston*, 77–79.
5. Dickerman, *House of Plant*, 106.
6. Ibid., 102–12.
7. Frasier, *Patriots, Pistols, and Petticoats*, 141–42.
8. Ellet, *Women of the American Revolution*, 306–07.
9. Dickerman, *House of Plant*, 102–12.
10. RMC Book K-6, 347–48.
11. Edgar, *South Carolina Encyclopedia*, 408.
12. RMC Book N-9, 470.
13. RMC Book V-13, 544
14. RMC Book V-17, 378.
15. RMC Book E-15, 527.

16. RMC Book K-19, 286.

17. Poston, *Buildings of Charleston*, 78–79.

THE PATRIOT

18. Dickerman, *House of Plant*, 196.

19. Salley, *Journal of the Commissioners*, 3, 6–8, 11–13, 15–16, 20, 76–77.

20. *South Carolina Gazette*, March 14, 1780.

21. McCrady, *South Carolina in the Revolution*, 857.

22. Garden, *Anecdotes of the Revolutionary War*, 266.

23. Josiah Smith's diary, reproduced in *South Carolina Historical and Genealogical Magazine*

24. Dickerman, *House of Plant*, 126.

25. Ver Steeg, *Robert Morris*, 102.

26. Young, *Forgotten Patriot*, 101.

27. McCrady, *South Carolina in the Revolution*, 678–79.

28. Young, *Forgotten* Patriot, 145–146.

29. Uhlendorf, *Siege of Charleston*.

30. Garden, *Anecdotes of the Revolutionary War*, 269–70. Some of Garden's story varies from other sources.

31. McCrady, *South Carolina in the Revolution*, 304–308; Leland, "Lowndes Grove"; and Stockton, "Former Plantation House."

32. Dickerman, *House of Plant*, 112.

INVASION OF PEACEFUL RETREAT

33. Rivers, et al., *Mendel and Me*, 38; and Edgar, *South Carolina Encyclopedia*, 372.

34. Mary Anna Gibbes married Major Alexander Garden after the Revolution and he wrote of her heroic rescue; however, Ellet's chronicle disputes some of the details in Garden's account. See Garden, *Anecdotes of the Revolutionary War*, 229–30.

35. Dickerman, *House of Plant*, 190.

36. Ravenel, *Piazza Tales*, 22.
37. Ellet, *Women of the American Revolution*, 308–09; Dickerman, *House of Plant*, 190; and Ravenel, *Piazza Tales*, 22.

Shipwrecked

38. Edgar, *South Carolina Encyclopedia*, 792.
39. Horner, *Blockade Runners*, 102–03.
40. C.F. Middleton letter, July 3, 1864.
41. Hamilton, *Blockade Runners of the Confederacy*, 290–91; and Horner, *Blockade Runners*, 106–09.
42. Horner, *Blockade Runners*, 108–09.
43. Middleton Letter, September 30, 1864.
44. Bradlee, *Blockade Running During the Civil War*.

High Cotton

45. Porter, *Led On!*, 236–37.
46. Rivers et al., *Mendel and Me*, 36–37, 42.

Change in Family Fortunes

47. Poston, *Buildings of Charleston*, 541.
48. Hasell, *Baynard*, 166.

The Odious Mr. Mackey

49. Poston, *Buildings of Charleston*, 319–20
50. Baggett, *The Scalawags*, 226.
51. Williams, *Hampton and His Red Shirts*, 369.
52. Wellman, *Giant in Gray*, 274–78.

Tootin' the Boul

53. Poston, *Buildings of Charleston*, 314.
54. Ibid., 223.

SCANDAL ON MEETING STREET

55. Ravenel, *Charleston.*
56. Frasier, *Charleston! Charleston!*, 23.
57. Ibid., 173–75.
58. Rivers et al., *Mendel and Me*, 32.
59. Anne Hyde, daughter of Elizabeth Waring, correspondence, September 2007.
60. Yarborough, *Passion for Justice*, 36.
61. Ibid., 30–31.
62. Rivers et al., *Mendel and Me*, 88–89.
63. Yarborough, *Passion for Justice*, 41.

CLOSING THE DOOR ON AN ERA

64. Poston, *Buildings of Charleston* , 219, 291.
65. Ravenel, *Piazza Tales*, 19.
66. Ibid., 23–24.
67. Ibid., 6.
68. Ibid., 67–69.
69. Ibid., 88–89.
70. Ibid., 140–43.
71. Stockton, *The Great Shock*, 41.
72. Located in Greenville, Delaware, Winterthur is the ancestral home of Henry Francis Du Pont. It has the finest collection of American decorative arts in the world. Du Pont purchased paneling from a dismantled house located at 71 Broad Street that was once the home of William Ward Burrows, appointed by President John Adams to be the second major commandant of the Marine Corps. This paneling is now in Winterthur's "Charleston Room." Du Pont tried to purchase the paneling from the great center hall at Drayton Hall. Although the money would have come in handy during the Depression, the Drayton sisters flatly refused his offer.

BIBLIOGRAPHY

Baggett, James Alex. *The Scalawags*. Baton Rouge: Louisiana State University Press, 2002.

Bradlee, Francis B.C. *Blockade Running During the Civil War*. Salem, MA: Newcomb & Gauss. Reprinted in *Historical Collections of the Essex Institute*. Vols. LX and LXI. 1925.

Brown, S. *The Loss of the* Lelia. Private paper now in the College of Charleston Special Collections Library (Rivers Family Papers).

Dickerman, G.S. *House of Plant*. New Haven, CT: Tuttle, Morehouse & Taylor Company, 1900.

Doughtie, Beatrice Mackey. *The Mackeys and Allied Families*. Decatur, GA: Bowen Press, Inc., 1957.

Edgar, Walter, ed. *The South Carolina Encyclopedia*. Columbia: University of South Carolina Press, 2006.

Ellet, Elizabeth F. *The Women of the American Revolution*. "Sarah Reeve Gibbes," Philadelphia: George W. Jacobs and Company, reprint 2004.

Frasier, Walter, J. *Charleston! Charleston! The History of a Southern City*. Columbia: University of South Carolina Press, 1989.

———. *Patriots, Pistols, and Petticoats*. Columbia, SC: R.L. Bryan Company, 1976.

Garden, Alexander. *Anecdotes of the Revolutionary War*. Spartanburg, SC: The Reprint Company, 1972.

Gibbes, A. Mason. "Distinguished Richlander: James Hopkins Adams, 1812–1861: A Paper to Be Read to the Forum Club, Columbia, SC, March 7, 1968." Citing the following works: Carnathan, W.J. Unnamed article in *South Atlantic Quarterly* (1926); Easterby, J.H. (work not named); Hollis (work not named); Perry, Benjamin Franklin. *Reminiscences of Public Men.* N.d.; Scott, Edwin J. *Random Recollections of a Long Life.* N.d.

Hamilton, Cochran. *Blockade Runners of the Confederacy.* New York: The Bobbs-Merrill Company, Inc., 1959.

Hasell, Annie Baynard Simons. *Baynard: An Ancient Family Bearing Arms.* Columbia, SC: R.L. Bryan Company, 1970.

Horner, Dave. *The Blockade Runners.* Cornwall, NY: The Cornwall Press, Inc., 1968.

Hyde, Anne. Correspondence, September 2007. College of Charleston Special Collections Library, Rivers Family Papers, Charleston, SC.

Leland, Jack. "Lowndes Grove has Long and Distinguished History." *Charleston News & Courier*, February 10, 1966.

McCrady, Edward, LLD. *South Carolina in the Revolution 1775–1780.* Norwood, MA: The Macmillan Company, Norwood Press, 1902.

———. *South Carolina in the Revolution 1780–1783.* Norwood, MA: The Macmillan Company, Norwood Press, 1902.

Middleton, Charles Francis. "Family Letters of My Great Grandfather." *Bermuda Historical Quarterly* 28, no. 4 (Winter 1971).

Middleton, Margaret Simons. *Live Oak Plantation.* Charleston, SC: Nelsons' Southern Printing and Publishing Company, 1956.

Obituary of Charles F. Middleton. *Charleston News & Courier*, October 13, 1939.

Porter, A. Toomer. *Led On! Step by Step.* 100th anniversary edition. New York: Arno Press, 1967.

Poston, Jonathan H. *The Buildings of Charleston, A Guide to the City's Architecture.* Columbia: University of South Carolina Press, 1997.

Ravenel, Mrs. St. Julien. *Charleston, The Place and the People*. New York: The McMillan Company, 1912.

Ravenel, Rose Pringle. *Piazza Tales*. Private printing, 2007.

Register of Mesne Conveyance (RMC). 101 Meeting Street, Charleston, SC.

Rivers Margaret M. *Fanfan*. Charleston, SC: The Nelson Printing Corporation, 1984.

Rivers, Margaret Middleton, et al. *Mendel and Me*. Charleston, SC: The History Press, 2007.

Salley, A.S., ed. *Journal of the Commissioners of the Navy of South Carolina, October 9, 1776–March 1, 1779*. Columbia, SC: The Historical Commission of South Carolina by The State Company, 1912.

Stockton, Robert P. "Former Plantation House Surrounded by Legend." *Charleston News & Courier*, August 25, 1975. 1-B.

———. *The Great Shock*. Easley, SC: Southern Historical Press, Inc., 1986.

Trott Family Papers. College of Charleston Special Collections Library, Unprocessed Good Family Papers, Charleston, SC.

Uhlendorf, Bernhard A. *The Siege of Charleston. With an account of the province of South Carolina; the diaries and letters of Hessian soldiers from the von Junkeen papers*. Unknown binding, 1938.

Ver Steeg, C.L. *Robert Morris: Revolutionary Financier*. Philadelphia: University of Pennsylvania Press, 1954.

Wellman, Manly Wade. *Giant in Gray*. New York: Charles Scribner's Sons, 1949.

Williams, Alfred B. *Hampton and His Red Shirts, South Carolina's Deliverance in 1876*. Charleston, SC: Walker, Evans & Cogswell Company, 1935.

Willis, Eola, *The Charleston Theatre in the XVIII Century*. Columbia, SC: The State Company, 1924.

Yarborough, Tinsley E. *A Passion for Justice, J. Waties Waring and Civil Rights*. New York: Oxford University Press, 1987.

Young, Eleanor May. *Forgotten Patriot: Robert Morris*. Unknown binding, 1950.

ABOUT THE AUTHOR

Margaret (Peg) M.R. Eastman was born in Charleston, South Carolina, and has family ties that date back to the original English and French settlers in the Carolinas. Active in church and civic activities, she also enjoys renovating houses, gardening, cooking, decorating, writing and lecturing. With her Charleston background, she has an interest in history and was a professional guide at Winterthur Museum, in Greenville, Delaware, the finest collection of American decorative arts in the world. She coauthored *Mendel and Me: Life with Congressman L. Mendel Rivers,* a book about her father, as well as a textbook on job documentation published by McGraw-Hill. She was a partner in a consulting business that required extensive travel both in and out of the United States, and she particularly liked visiting the Canadian Rockies and Alaska. Her two married sons are both former Reconnaissance Marines; one is now an attorney specializing in veterans law and the other is an ER physician. She currently resides in Charleston, South Carolina.